The
Garland Library
of
War and Peace

The
Garland Library
of
War and Peace

Under the General Editorship of
Blanche Wiesen Cook, *John Jay College, C.U.N.Y.*
Sandi E. Cooper, *Richmond College, C.U.N.Y.*
Charles Chatfield, *Wittenberg University*

Military Training

comprising

Military Training in Schools and Colleges f the United States
by
Winthrop D. Lane

Universal Military Training
Our Latest Cure-All
by
Oswald Garrison Villard

Universal Military Training and Democracy
by
George Nasmyth

Militarizing Our Youth
by
Roswell P. Barnes
with an introduction
by
John Dewey

So This is War!
by
Tucker P. Smith

with a new introduction
for the Garland Edition by

E. Raymond Wilson

Garland Publishing, Inc., New York & London

1971

The new introduction for this
Garland Library Edition is Copyright © 1971, by
Garland Publishing Inc.
24 West 45 St., New York, N.Y. 10036

Library of Congress Cataloging in Publication Data
Main entry under title:

Military training.

    (The Garland library of war and peace)
    Includes bibliographical references.
    CONTENTS: Military training in schools and colleges
of the United States, by W. D. Lane [first published
1925].--Universal military training, by O. G. Villard
[first published 1918].--Universal military training
and democracy, by G. Nasmyth [first published 1919].
[etc.]
    1. Military education--U. S.--Addresses, essays,
lectures. I. Title. II. Series.
U408.M55 1972   355.02'13   72-149525

ISBN 0-8240-0417-5

Printed in the United States of America

Introduction

Lester Pearson used to say that humanity is like a giant in preparing for war but like a pigmy in preparing for peace. The figure has been lamentably appropriate to our schools and colleges.

A bill requiring three months of compulsory military training of all eighteen- or nineteen-year-old boys was introduced in Congress scarcely three months after the close of World War I, the war which allegedly was "to end war." The measure was endorsed by Secretary of War Newton D. Baker. It aroused many peace advocates who had organized to fight American military preparedness before the war and intervention in it, and whose organizations had been left much in disarray as a result of the war effort.

The American Union Against Militarism (AUAM) was one such organization. Formed in 1915-1916 by a group of notable progressives who were apprehensive of the impact of militarism upon democratic reform, the AUAM had been weakened during the war by divided counsel within and by patriotic conformism from without. Its remaining leaders sensed a renewed threat in peacetime conscription. They found also a focal point upon which, they thought, a reunited peace movement could meet the public on the ground of established national values. Its executive committee voted to concentrate on that issue. It established a lobby in Washington and arranged for the publication of anti-conscription literature.

The chairman of the executive committee was Oswald Garrison Villard (1872-1949), who had inherited much of the civil liberties fervor of his abolitionist grandfather, William Lloyd Garrison. A founder and for a time chairman of the executive committee of the N.A.A.C.P., he wrote a sympathetic biography of John Brown *(1910). Beginning in 1918, he converted* The Nation *from a tradition-bound literary magazine into a vigorous liberal forum with which he was associated for nearly a half-century, as editor through 1932. When he finally severed ties with his journal he wrote in a valedictory (June 29, 1940) that its chief glory had been its "steadfast opposition to all war; to universal military service, to a great navy, and to all war."*

He had established his own opposition to militarism in his 1918 pamphlet, Universal Military Training: Our Latest Cure-All. *His outrage at the prospect of peacetime conscription was a positive assertion of his commitment to civil liberties and a reflection of his defense of them during the oppressive war years. Beyond that, he appealed for a constructive, progressive approach to world responsibility. He concluded: "No, to lead the world aright, the United States ought not to be debating whether it prefers voluntary military training or universal conscription, but how rapidly it can induce the other nations by precept, by example, by enlightened leadership, to limit their armaments to the dimensions of police forces." His appeal would be still largely unheeded in 1971.*

George Nasmyth (1882-1920) wrote another pamphlet under the auspices of the AUAM, Universal Military Training and Democracy. *Like Villard, he responded both to the threat to civil liberties and to the wasted opportunity for constructive internationalism implicit in what he regarded as American militarism. He had earned a Ph.D. at Cornell University in 1909 and had studied in German universities for the following three years. He had been instrumental in organizing the Cosmopolitan Club movement; and he had been a director of the World Peace Federation, secretary of the Massachusetts branch of the League to Enforce Peace, and a press representative at the Paris Peace Conference.*

A sociologist and internationalist, he was well prepared to argue that the adoption in the United States of the European system of conscription would not promote democracy, good discipline, or national unity. Militarism has been the most formidable enemy of democracy everywhere, he wrote. Discipline enforced by authority breaks down as soon as the restraining force is removed. In a democracy discipline must spring from an inner commitment to national values. He concluded that America was the

7

only great nation left in the world in which militarism was not enthroned through the principle of conscription. Like Villard, he asked: Shall the last fortress of democracy and the greatest adventure in human history go down in a failure of nerve?

As if in answer to this question, universal military training was omitted from the Army Act of June 4, 1920. Shortly afterward the AUAM suspended its activities, deferring to other groups organized to promote disarmament. Military training in public schools and colleges was encouraged under the National Defense Acts of 1916 and 1920, however, so that by the middle of the nineteen-twenties peace advocates found themselves engaged in an extended campaign against the Reserve Officers Training Corps. That program was mandatory in eighty-six colleges and universities by 1927, elective in forty-four others, and was implemented in high schools in over fifty cities.

That was the context in which I was introduced to the peace movement. I had served in the navy in World War I, and had been challenged to think about pacifism for the first time in 1923 when Kirby Page addressed a National Student Volunteers Conference in Indianapolis. In 1925 I was a graduate student at Teachers College, Columbia University, when John Nevin Sayre and Norman Thomas asked me to spend a quarter of my time helping them to organize a Committee on Militarism in Education (CME) and to circulate a pamphlet written by Winthrop D. Lane at

INTRODUCTION

their urging. It proved to be a nearly full-time task: helping to edit the pamphlet, lining up fifty-four distinguished citizens to sign it, and planning for the initial circulation of over 100,000 copies. Indeed, I never completed my dissertation but launched instead on a career in peace work that took me from the Committee on Militarism in Education to the Friends Committee on National Legislation.

The Committee worked for the abolition of all military training in high schools and for the elimination of compulsory military training in colleges and universities until, with the advent of conscription again, it disbanded in 1940. In the process of seeking limited goals, however, the Committee promulgated the basic view that, in the words of those persons who endorsed the Lane pamphlet, it is "alien to the best interests of our universities and to the highest ideals of learning that the War Department should be given so much power and military training so much place as it now has in our college world." The conviction, more than the specific objectives of the CME, provoked the abuse heaped upon its leaders by military-minded patriots who attacked us as communist-pinks and pacifist-traitors. We experienced then what another generation would feel in the McCarthy Era, the innuendo of fanatics who made a profession of attacking those who wanted to shift the emphasis in the United States from militarism to a genuine search for international organization and peace.

9

INTRODUCTION

That was one reason that we were so careful with our facts and arguments that after two months of circulation only two minor errors had been reported in the pioneering Lane pamphlet. Another reason for our care was the breadth of spirit and integrity of purpose of the founders, especially John Nevin Sayre and Norman Thomas.

Although Thomas (1884-1968) had not yet reached the commanding level of leadership that he would exert in the thirties, already he was a recognized spokesman for the American conscience. John Nevin Sayre (1884-) was the godfather and leading proponent of the Committee on Militarism in Education. Educated at Princeton and ordained in the Episcopal Church, he had been a missionary in China before World War I. He resigned his pastorate in Suffern, New York, after the war to help found The Brookwood School, and early in the twenties he was editor of The World Tomorrow, *a vigorous magazine of the Social Gospel. Sayre was the pivotal figure in the pacifist Fellowship of Reconciliation (FOR) in America between the wars, and he traveled all over the world encouraging lonely pacifists in country after country and raising funds with which to sustain their international organization. He brought to the Committee on Militarism in Education the vision of a world where schools would be free from the repressive menace of militarism.*

He brought to the Committee, also, Roswell P. Barnes, who became its full-time secretary in the

INTRODUCTION

summer of 1926. Barnes later held various church positions, including that of Associate Secretary of the Commission on International Justice and Goodwill of the Federal Council of Churches, and before his retirement he was the United States representative of the World Council of Churches. A pacifist and FOR member, Barnes wrote a sequel to the Lane pamphlet which was published in 1927: Militarizing Our Youth.

Summarizing the situation then, he sketched the rapid growth of the Reserve Officers Training Corps (R.O.T.C.). In the previous fifteen years federal spending for military training in civil schools had increased from \$725,168 to \$10,696,504, a fifteen-fold increase; the number of institutions giving such training had quadrupled, from 57 to 223; the army personnel detailed to conduct it had multiplied by twenty-one, from 85 to 1809; and the number of students enrolled had grown fourfold from 29,979 to 119,914.

The program would continue to expand until by October 31, 1970 the number of colleges and universities would total 347 with an R.O.T.C. enroll-ment of 109,598. There would be 871 high schools with military training involving 130,652 students; and the National Defense Cadet Corps, with a program somewhat similar to R.O.T.C., would enroll 29 high schools with 3785 students. Actual appropriations for the fiscal year ending June 30, 1970 would be \$48,297,000 for Army, Navy, and Air Force units, a sum about five times the appropriation for the Arms

11

Control and Disarmament Agency, charged with seeking an end to the arms race.

Had Barnes foreseen these developments he would have predicted dire consequences for the Republic, for he pictured the R.O.T.C. system as an invidious threat to its democratic base. He quoted R.O.T.C. manuals to demonstrate that the objectives of the system were to condition boys to respond to established authority and to kill upon command: "this inherent desire to fight and kill must be carefully watched for and encouraged by the instructor," a manual said. He described a War Department design to mold the "on-coming generation" in its image of citizenship. He documented a threat to freedom of discussion, exposing the propoganda of the national fraternity of the R.O.T.C., Scabbard and Blade, which described those advocating peace based on internationalism as subversive, communistic, and dangerous. All this, he urged, was evidence of a "well-organized movement to militarize the tone and temper of our national life." There was nothing frivolous about military training, according to Barnes, and under his leadership the CME sponsored vigorous opposition to it.

I left the Committee in the summer of 1926 in order to study in Japan on a Japanese Brotherhood Scholarship, the first American student sponsored by Japanese students in the United States. I returned to the struggle a few years later through the Pennsylvania Committee on Militarism in Education, which was fighting compulsory R.O.T.C. at Penn State College. In the fall of 1930 I worked in the state-wide campaign in Iowa to eliminate compulsory military training at Iowa State College and the State University of Iowa. Our campaign failed, largely because we could not convince the state legislature of widespread student opposition to the program. I returned to work with the national office in New York until the financial crisis led to my resignation, effective September 1, 1931. By then I had come to know well the new secretary of the CME, Tucker P. Smith.

A former general secretary of the Y.M.C.A., Tucker Smith was a socialist, an officer in the FOR and the War Resisters League, the executive director of the League for Industrial Democracy, and the director of Brookwood Labor College. After World War II he would become secretary of the Y.M.C.A. at New York University.

He was a dynamic individual who had experience in labor organizing and street speaking, but who also set aside time early each morning for serious reading so that he acquired a wide range of knowledge. He was imaginative on his feet. I recall a demonstration in which a group of laborers confronted National Guardsmen who had been called to the scene of a strike. The situation was very tense. Tucker Smith strode to the captain of the National Guard and said, "There's going to be violence here unless you fellows stack your arms. I am asking you to stack your arms, and I will disarm the strikers." The captain called his men together and they stacked their arms. And Tucker went up and down the lines of strikers gathering up the baseball bats, bottles, and stones, and thus averted violence which easily could have led to bloodshed.

He brought that courage and imagination which he had to the CME. He brought, too, his penchant for vigorous research, writing, and speaking, and his broad range of experience. And he brought a sense of satire with which he made the R.O.T.C. look not so much menacing as ridiculous. Thus, in So This is War! *he showed how the attempt to popularize the program eliminated the realism of military life, how it was sweetened with pretty girl officers and sponsors, girl rifle teams, parades and reviews, sham battles and war games, prizes and awards, riding and polo horses. It was all true and, however frivolous, sad. As I pointed out in the Iowa campaign in 1930, the War Department was spending more money for hay and feed for the horses in the military unit on the campus of my alma mater, Iowa State College, than the college was spending on salaries for professors who taught courses on international relations and ways and means of achieving peace.*

That was what the Committee on Militarism in Education was all about. It never had much money. It skated from dollar to dollar, carrying on a persistent effort on campuses and in legislative halls to put military training in the perspective of the twentieth-

INTRODUCTION

century world and a democratic republic. Our basic argument was that we needed to train for the difficulties and complexities of peace rather than to put our emphasis on squads right and squads left.

It was a lonely, uphill battle against an entrenched military system about which most people seemed unconcerned. If it had been successful, it would have prevented much of the tension over R.O.T.C. that occurs in many colleges and universities now. These tensions are symptomatic of a failure that is only symbolized by the presence of R.O.T.C. units. More basic is the failure of educators to provide a coherent alternative to military training. While there has been a vast increase of emphasis and discussion in the educational world since the campaigns of the Committee on Militarism in Education, there still is not the leadership from higher education that is needed to match the demands of our time — when the arms race is on the verge of defying control, when the nuclear age has brought into the hands of the military unparalleled capacity for destruction, when the world is polarized between various idological camps, and when war itself has become a more serious enemy than any other country.

E. Raymond Wilson
*Executive Secretary Emeritus of the
Friends Committee on National Legislation
Wittenberg University*

MILITARY TRAINING

IN
SCHOOLS AND COLLEGES
OF THE
UNITED STATES

༃

The Facts and an Interpretation

༃

By
WINTHROP D. LANE

This "account....will, we think, come as a surprise
to many Americans....Facts like these call for some
action."

—From the Foreword, signed by Miss Jane
Addams, Senator Wm. E. Borah, Prof. John
Dewey, Bishop Francis J. McConnell, Rabbi Stephen S. Wise and more than fifty other prominent Americans.

CITIES IN WHICH THERE ARE HIGH SCHOOLS WITH RESERVE OFFICERS' TRAINING CORPS †

Compulsory	Elective
Athens, Ga.	Alameda, Calif.
California Polytechnic, San Luis Obispo, Calif.*	Atlanta, Ga.
Canon City, Colo.	Bangor, Me.
Chattanooga, Tenn.	Beloit, Wis.
Cheyenne, Wyo.	Birmingham, Ala.
Council Bluffs, Iowa.	Boise, Idaho.
Gloucester, Mass.	Calumet, Mich.
Griffin, Ga.	Chicago, Ill.
Knoxville, Tenn.	Cleveland, O.
Louisville, Ky.	Dallas, Texas.
Macon, Ga.	Davenport, Iowa.
Memphis, Tenn.	Detroit, Mich.
Nashville, Tenn.	El Paso, Texas.
Ogden, Utah.	Fort Worth, Texas.
Owensboro, Ky.	Gary, Ind.
Ontario, Oregon.*	Grand Rapids, Mich.
Park City, Utah.*	Indianapolis. Ind.
Sacramento, Calif.*	Joliet, Ill.
Salt Lake City, Utah.	Joplin, Mo.
San Diego, Calif.	Kansas City, Mo.
Santa Barbara, Calif.	Leavenworth, Kan.
St. Joseph, Mo.	Long Branch, Calif.
Walla Walla, Wash.	Los Angeles, Calif.
	Montgomery, Ala.
	New Bedford. Mass.
	Oakland, Calif.
	Pasadena, Calif.
	Reno, Nevada.
	Riverside, Calif.
	Rockford, Ill.
	San Antonio, Texas.
	San Francisco, Calif.
	Waukegan, Ill.

† Compiled from data supplied by the War Department to House Committee having in charge War Department Appropriation Bill for 1926, pp. 603-607. Information on compulsory feature secured by correspondence with Commanders of Corps Areas and Superintendents of Schools.

* Organized not as R. O. T. C. units but under Section 55-c of The National Defense Act.

FOREWORD

Mr. Lane's account of the extent of military training in the United States will, we think, come as a surprise to many Americans. His conclusions are so well founded on facts that they do not need recommendation from anyone. They carry their own weight to the thoughtful reader.

But facts like these call for some action. Even those who, having read this pamphlet, still believe in the R. O. T. C., will surely want to be on their guard against its becoming a means of militarizing America. It would be a tragedy if at the very moment when such ancient enemies as France and Germany are outlawing war between each other, the military spirit should assert itself in the United States.

Our schools ought to be the best defense against this. There, certainly, we should have a positive education for peace. Such education is wholly inconsistent (1) with military training in the *high schools,* and (2) with *compulsory* military training in the colleges.

At the very least, military training should be rigidly excluded from the high schools. It does not provide the best form of physical training, it does not teach constructive citizenship; if successful it tends to impart aggressive, even jingoistic, notions by its effect upon immature minds at their formative period. When such training is made compulsory in high schools it is an indirect approach to that universal military training and service which in peace time public opinion in America has overwhelmingly rejected.

The same argument applies to compulsory military training in the colleges when imposed by college faculties. A country which has refused to accept compulsory training and service for all its citizens cannot consistently permit young men ambitious for an education to be forced into accepting military training as part of the price for that education.

So much ought to be clear to every man who has respect for the spirit of American institutions and hope for American leadership in world peace. The removal of military training from high schools, and of its compulsory feature from the colleges, is a minimum program for dealing with the R. O. T. C. But a

3

further conclusion is forced upon us. We are convinced that it is alien to the best interests of our universities and to the highest ideals of learning that the War Department should be given so much power, and military training so much place as it now has, in our college world. The atmosphere of military training is not the atmosphere for the finest, the most thoughtful work along any line requiring independent thinking. Higher education ought to exist for the encouragement of independent thinking. Science, art, and culture are not and cannot be purely national. All learning is witness to the truth that "above all nations is humanity." Colleges and universities, therefore, are peculiarly inappropriate fields for military training and for the intrusive presence of a military bureaucracy. We Americans would have said this of any country in the world. There is no virtue of our own which makes us immune to a militarism which has played so fatal a role in Europe.

In recommending this pamphlet, therefore, we urge not merely thoughtful consideration of its statements but action to secure to American youth such educational influences as will make unequivocally for peace.

(SIGNED):

Jane Addams
Will W. Alexander
Leslie Blanchard
Wm. E. Borah
Benjamin Brewster
John Brophy
Carrie Chapman Catt
Samuel Cavert
Francis E. Clarke
George A. Coe
Henry Sloane Coffin
Albert F. Coyle
John Dewey
Paul H. Douglas
W. E. Burghardt DuBois
Sherwood Eddy
Charles A. Ellwood
Zona Gale
Charles M. Gilkey

Thomas Que Harrison
Harold A. Hatch
Stanley High
George Huddleston
Hannah Clothier Hull
James Weldon Johnson
Rufus M. Jones
Paul U. Kellogg
Wm. H. Kilpatrick
Robert M. LaFollette, Jr.
Halford E. Luccock
Frederick Lynch
Henry N. MacCracken
Irving Maurer
James H. Maurer
Francis J. McConnell
Orie O. Miller
Charles Clayton Morrison
Samuel K. Mosiman
Mary E. Wooley

John M. Nelson
George W. Norris
Edward L. Parsons
Kirby Page
George Foster Peabody
David R. Porter
Francis B. Sayre
John Nevin Sayre
J. Henry Scattergood
Joseph Schlossberg
Charles M. Sheldon
Henrik Shipstead
Abba Hillel Silver
John F. Sinclair
William E. Sweet
Wilbur K. Thomas
Henry P. Van Dusen
Oswald G. Villard
Stephen S. Wise

Military Training in Schools and Colleges of the United States.

The Surprising Thing That Is Happening.

MILITARY training confronts the young men of the United States today on a scale that it has never before reached. Under the encouragement of the War Department, it is being rapidly extended and is becoming a prominent part of the education offered by civilian schools and colleges. Most people do not know how far this has gone. A large number of educational institutions that had no military training five years ago have it today. In many of these it is compulsory. That is, all young men are required to take it.

Educational institutions in which it now exists are some of the best known schools in the land, colleges famous on the football field and in one form or another of academic achievement. The list is not by any means confined to land grant colleges, which have long had a greater or less measure of military science and neither does it stop with colleges. It includes high schools where boys of fourteen years and over, many of whom are still in knee pants, parade in uniform, take lessons in rifle marksmanship and learn the ways of military guard duty, scouting and patrolling.

A War Department Drive.

The training hereinafter described is not the result of chance or of the action of local school or public officials. It is not the mere contagion of a purpose temporarily in the minds of many people. It is encouraged, supervised and regulated by the War Department. The purpose is to make soldiers. It is not training in citizenship, or any vague and ill-defined training of a general military nature. The official object is to "provide systematic military training at civil educational institutions for the purpose of qualifying selected students of such institutions for appointment as reserve officers in the military forces of the United States."

The courses of study used in these schools are written and supplied by the War Department. Their use is prescribed. No school can receive the benefit of War Department assistance if it does not use these courses. Moreover, the War Department, authorized by law, specifies the number of hours that students

5

must spend on this military training. Credits toward graduation are conferred by colleges that give it.

MILITARY FACULTIES OF TWENTY.

Assistance rendered by the War Department to schools is substantial. Uniforms worn by students are supplied by it; so, also, is all necessary equipment. The War Department pays students in the senior (or college) division of military training sums in cash sufficient to subsidize the last two years of college education for many a boy in difficult circumstances. Moreover, it supplies the men who teach these youths. . To each school the War Department assigns an officer of the Regular Army as "professor of military science and tactics." It supplies his assistants, —other officers of the Regular Army. The military science faculty in Ohio State University numbers twenty and in the University of Illinois twenty-two—all assigned and paid by the War Department. This number is equal in size to the entire faculty of many a smaller college.

Neither is the War Department content with training boys and young men at school. It has established Citizens' Military Training Camps, or the C. M. T. C., as they are called, for lads who have left school and gone to work. In the summer of 1925 there were twenty-eight camps and Congress appropriated $2,100,-000 for their support. The citizen's military training camps really began in 1921, though there had been pre-war and war camps for training soldiers before that. The real post-war C. M. T. C. has been going, however, for only five years. In 1921 the number of young men in attendance was 10,681, in 1922 it rose to 22,000, in 1923 to 25,000 and in 1924 the number was 34,000. "The time is not far distant," wrote General Pershing this past summer, "when, instead of training 35,000 young men, we will be training 100,000 each year."*

So rapid has been the growth of military training that few people are aware of what has actually taken place. The accomplishment of the War Department, and its avowed policy, are such as to raise this question. Is it the purpose of the Federal Government, working through the War Department, to bring about universal military training for boys fourteen years of age and older in the schools of the United States? And this further question is pertinent: Does Congress wish to support this program?

* From a newspaper article signed by General Pershing and syndicated. This was one of a series of six such articles. The extract quoted can be found in *The Minneapolis Morning Tribune*, July 17, 1925.

6

HAVE WE CHANGED OUR OPINION?

It is safe to say that, when the United States entered the war in 1917—and earlier, in 1915 and 1916—most people in this country conceived German militarism to be the enemy that we were fighting. No other conception could have given rise to the cry that we were going into the war to "make the world safe for democracy". That militarism was believed to be extraordinary preparation for, and concentration on, war. We thought that the war was due in no small part to this pre-occupation with the military purpose and method. We believed then that no nation that required all of its young men to take training as soldiers could be regarded as strongly devoted to peace. We believed that militarism was in some way closely bound up with this universal, or almost universal, military service and training. Have we changed our opinion?

President Coolidge in a speech before the graduating class of the U. S. Naval Academy, June 3, 1925, said: "I am not unfamiliar with the claim that if only we had a sufficient military establishment no one would ever molest us. I know of no nation in history that has ever been able to attain that position. I see no reason to expect that we could be the exception." And in an address before the American Legion, Oct. 6, 1925, he said: "The real question is whether spending more money to make a better military force would really make a better country." The preparation of American schoolboys to be soldiers and officers is both adding to the American military establishment and spending more money on military forces. It is not only an aggrandizement of the military arm, but it is training these boys to think in terms of war purposes and military spirit.

WHY THIS PAMPHLET HAS BEEN WRITTEN.

The object of this pamphlet is to put facts into the hands of the American people. The public has not passed upon the question of military training for youth. It has registered opposition to the idea of universal compulsory military training, but upon the present near-substitute it has not spoken. Congress, under the emotion of a great European war, put into effect the National Defense Act, and in so doing authorized the President of the United States to introduce military training into civil educational institutions: the War Department is now showing what this may mean, but the general public has hardly known what was going on.

How did Military Training Get Started?

Now how did the thing get going? Nearly everyone knows that there are in the United States what are called "land grant colleges". These were established in pursuance of an act of Congress passed in 1862, called the Morrill Land Grant Act. This gave land to the states on condition that they establish colleges devoted primarily to teaching agriculture and the mechanic arts. Nearly every state in the union now has one such college. The state agricultural college is in most states the land grant institution, though in some the state university is. The law required that military training be offered in these colleges. All land grant schools have, therefore, ever since offered some form of military instruction to their students, but in many, if not in most, this was little more than a kind of military physical drill and was not taken seriously by the military authorities of the Government of the United States.

All this was changed, however, in 1916, when the European War raised the enthusiasm, and stirred the fears, of military people in this country. That was the year of the great "preparedness" drive, when the country was swept by appeals to increase the money spent on defenses, augment the army and prepare for war in other ways. The idea of universal military training was put forward. The instrument was the National Defense Act. Though passed first in 1916, its provisions in regard to military education were not closely drawn, but in 1920 this Act was amended and enlarged so that it became the legislative base from which the military people executed their drive on the schools.

The R. O. T. C.

This act authorizes the President to establish and maintain in "civil educational institutions" a Reserve Officers' Training Corps. This corps is to consist of various units or branches, infantry, cavalry, field artillery, signal corps, medical and others. In any given school there may be one or more units of this corps. The corps is to be established only in schools having at least 100 physically fit male students under military instruction, except that 50 may be the minimum in units other than infantry, cavalry and artillery. No unit is to be set up in any school until an officer of the Regular Army has been detailed by the War Department to serve as "professor of military science and tactics" and until the authorities of the school agree to maintain, as a

8

minimum, a two years' course in military instruction. The law requires that such course, when entered upon by any student, must be a pre-requisite for graduation by him unless he be "relieved of this obligation by regulations to be prescribed by the Secretary of War."

The law further specifies that the Secretary of War shall have authority to prescribe standard courses of military training for these youths, and that no unit of the R. O. T. C. can exist in any school that does not incorporate these courses into its curriculum. An extraordinary innovation this, that an American civil educational institution should relinquish to the War Department control over part of its teaching. The amount of teaching time thus *farmed out* is specified by the National Defense Act to be at least three hours a week for the first two years and at least five hours a week during the third and fourth year advanced courses.

The R. O. T. C. as thus established is divided into Junior and Senior divisions. Junior divisions are those conducted in high schools and preparatory schools, and senior divisions are in colleges and universities and some essentially military schools. In the senior division the work is divided into two parts, the basic course and the advanced course. The basic course consists of training given during the first two years of a college term, and the advanced course of training received during the third and fourth years. Any student who enters upon the advanced course is required to agree in writing to continue in the R. O. T. C. for two subsequent years. He must also agree to attend one summer R. O. T. C. camp, either at the end of his third year in school or at the end of his fourth. The duration of this camp is six weeks.

Eligibility to receive this military instruction is limited to students who are citizens, who are "not less than fourteen years of age" and whose bodily condition indicates that they are physically fit to perform military duty, or will be, upon reaching military age. Here, as in the regular army, the War Department does not care to waste time and money on any but the physically fit, despite its announcements, quoted later, that better citizenship is the object of the instruction given.

By the National Defense Act the President is authorized to appoint as a reserve officer of the Army of the United States any graduate of the senior division whose work has been satisfactory. To receive such appointment the student must take an oath to serve the United States as reserve officer for at least five years from the date of his appointment. Under the authority of this section 3,392 young men were made second lieutenants in the Army of the United States at the end of the school year of 1924.

Many land grant colleges have established R. O. T. C. units under the provisions of this Act. This gives them a fuller measure of government support and better facilities for giving military training than they had under the Morrill Act.

The law further authorizes the Secretary of War to support military training at schools other than those maintaining the R. O. T. C. units. This it does under section 55c. The Secretary of War may issue arms, tents and other equipment, and may assign officers and enlisted men to teach youths, and may prescribe the courses of instruction just as he does for schools having units of the R. O. T. C.

How Many Schools Give Training?

During the last school year, that of 1924-25, military instruction was given in *more* than 226 educational institutions in the United States. The exact number is difficult to obtain. Two hundred and twenty-six institutions maintained units of the R. O. T. C., but as just explained, the Secretary of War encourages military training in schools which do not establish R. O. T. C. For the schools with R. O. T. C. Congress appropriated $3,818,-020 and the number of students taking military instruction was 125,504. To these schools the War Department assigned 768 officers and 1,064 enlisted men to carry on training; it paid their salaries. Before 1916 there were no R. O. T. C. units and the number of officers engaged in military in schools was only 119.

Of the 226 R. O. T. C. institutions in 1925, 124 were of college or university rank, 63 were high schools and 39 were what are known as "essentially military schools."*

Famous Colleges on the List.

It is interesting to note the names of some of these institutions. Many of the best known colleges in the land are on the list. Harvard, Yale, Princeton, Cornell, Leland Stanford, Johns Hopkins and the University of Pennsylvania are there; Northwestern

---

* The facts given with respect to the present extent of military training in R. O. T. C. units are taken from the published Hearings before the Subcommittee of House Committee on Appropriation in charge of the War Department Appropriation Bill for 1926; pp. 600-621.

University and the College of the City of New York are included. Nearly every state university in the country is on the list, including such famous ones as the University of Wisconsin, University of Michigan, University of Minnesota, Ohio State University and others. Among smaller colleges of high standing are Rutgers, Lehigh, Lafayette, Georgetown, Boston University and Western Reserve. The number includes many technical institutes, and practically all of the agricultural colleges. There is a large sprinkling of denominational and semi-denominational schools. In all of these colleges and universities military training is now an accepted reality.

High schools also in all parts of the country are giving military training. Among the cities where this is the case, are Cleveland, Washington, Chicago, Louisville, Kansas City, Indianapolis, San Francisco and Salt Lake City. There is drill in more than forty others. Youngsters of fourteen and older drill with rifles and learn the technique of guard duty and patrolling.

WHERE WILL THE WAR DEPARTMENT STOP?

The War Department does not plan to stop with what it has already done. Its purpose, apparently, is to go on, putting military training into one school after another, until all boys over fourteen years of age enrolled in the educational institutions of the United States are being drilled to take part in war.

John W. Weeks, Secretary of War, called a conference in the City of Washington in November, 1922, to discuss ways of "realizing more fully the provisions of the National Defense Act." To this conference were invited many boys' club leaders, educators, athletic directors and others who, in the opinion of the Secretary, might be helpful in bringing more and more youths under the influence of military training. One of the spokesmen for the War Department at this conference was Brig. Gen. William Lassiter. If the main purpose of the Reserve Officers' Training Corps, he said, were to produce reserve officers, then "our efforts should be especially directed towards the expansion both in the number of colleges reached and in students enrolled." If, on the other hand, the main purpose were to give the benefits of military instruction to a great number of boys and young men, then "the system ought to be expanded so as to give *all young men attending both schools and colleges* the opportunity of having this form of training and not confine it" to the institutions then maintaining such courses. Thus, whichever purpose was regarded as primary, the object was expansion. General Lassiter pointed out that "less

11

than one-fifth" of the colleges in the country of the United States had R. O. T. C. units at that time, and plainly intimated that the percentage should be raised. With respect to secondary schools he was even more explicit, declaring that there were "at least 1,200 secondary schools where junior units might be maintained." † (Italics ours.)

Another spokesman for the War Department, General Pershing, said that it was "our fervent hope" that out of the conference there held might come "plans and policies which could be applied to our public schools everywhere." And General Pershing made an even more significant remark. He seemed to see a substitute for universal military service in the R. O. T. C. and the C. M. T. C. "That we have not adopted the principle of universal military service," he said, "renders it highly essential that training which leads up to and, as far as possible, includes preparation for military service should be popularized by all available methods." In similar vein Secretary Weeks in an address at Lehigh University spoke of "the gradual development of the idea that it is the proper action for every self respecting young American to give a portion of his time during his youth to preparation for effective service if his country should ever need it."*

TRAINING FOR CITIZENSHIP—OR TO BE SOLDIERS?

A large part of military training, including the C. M. T. C., is sold to the public or to the college student by much talk about its being training for citizenship. It is better psychology to call it that than to say that it is training for war. Gen Pershing remarked that it must "be popularized by all available methods." Compare what is said concerning the R. O. T. C. to the American fathers and mothers, to army officers, and to students.

---

† —From Special Report of Secretary of War to the President on The Conference on Training for Citizenship and National Defense, 1922. pp. 8; 10.

* Address at Lehigh University, Oct. 8, 1921, quoted in pamphlet by Major General J. G. Harbord.

PRESENTING THE R. O. T. C.

To American Fathers and Mothers:

"The purpose of this book is *not to make soldiers out of your boys,* but to develop them physically, morally and mentally into the best type of citizens, capable of defending our flag should an emergency arise . . With the support of the parents we hope to get the American boy outdoors and enjoying these activities . . . which will develop that hardness and uprightness so common to the pioneers who founded this free country." (Italics ours.)

—From Preface to the Junior R. O. T. C. Manual, Page 5.

To Army Officers:

"Always remember that the men are the material being trained and moulded for the work of battle. They should be handled with the same care which an expert artisan gives a fine tool . . .

"So it is necessar" that a drill instructor look and act at all times on the drill field and elsewhere like a trained soldier, if he is to create in the minds of his men a desire to be like him. *They are being trained to be soldiers,* and the model should be actually before them." (Italics ours).

—From Infantry Drill Regulations for 1925 for Use with R. O. T. C. Manual, pp. 168 and 169.

To Students:

"*Success in battle,* whether attack or defense, is the aim of all military training. Everything that you have studied in this course, and everything that you will study in your further course of military training, has that great end in view—*success in battle, or victory."*

—The Junior R. O. T. C. Manual. Chap. XIV, pp. 499.

COURSES OF STUDY BY WAR DEPARTMENT

Physical training as well as citizenship is played up as an objective of C. M. T. C. and R. O. T. C. instruction. If one holds that military drill *per se* is good training in citizenship and physical culture there is perhaps some justification for this claim, but the public should then clearly realize that the "citizenship" and "physical training" thus spoken of are mostly synonymous with military instruction. The specific courses given in "citizenship" and "physical training" are practically negligible. An analysis of the War Department's division of students' time reveals the following:

1. R. O. T. C. in High Schools *

	Hours			
	1st year	2nd year	3rd year	4th year
Citizenship	0	0	0	
Physical Training	20	15	5	
Military Training and Instruction	76	81	91	

2. R. O. T. C. in Colleges †

Citizenship	0	0	0	0
Physical Training	6	0	0	0
Military Training and Instruction	90	96	160	160

3. Citizens Military Training Camps ‡

Citizenship	5	3	0	0
Physical Training	10	10	10	10
Hygiene and First Aid	5	3	0	0
Military Training and Instruction	90	104	126	148

It is thus evident that teaching in citizenship plays an insignificant part in the courses of instruction laid down by the War Department. Throughout the three years of the Junior R. O. T. C. unit no time is set aside for it; throughout the four years of the Senior R. O. T. C. unit, no time is so designated and throughout the four summers of the Citizens' Military Training Camp instruction, a grand total of 8 hours are devoted to citizenship. That is all. Similarly, physical training for 3 years of Junior R. O. T. C. receives a total of only 40 hours, in 4 years of Senior R. O. T. C. a total of only 6 hours and in 4 summers of C. M. T. C. a total of but 40 hours. The instruction all along the line is overwhelmingly devoted to out and out military subjects.

---

* Official Course of instruction and training for Junior Units of the R. O. T. C. Corps Established in Schools and Preparatory Departments other than essentially Military Schools. pp. 3-7.

† Official general instruction, Program of instruction and Training for Infantry Units of the Sr. Division R. O. T. C. pp. 2-6. Last two years in table refer to first and second year of advanced course.

‡ See War Department Training Program, Citizen's Military Training Camps, 1925, issued from office of the Adjutant General.

Opinions of Educators on Military Training.

Educators and others have frequently given their opinions on military training. Many of them are strongly against it. Its physical benefits, they point out, are over-rated; often it develops only certain muscles or some parts of the body, and does not do for young men what intelligently planned physical training does. Dudley A. Sargent, famous as the former director of the Hemenway Gymnasium at Harvard University, regards the drill that usually accompanies military training as "actually harmful" in many instances.

In regard to its "moral" or, more properly speaking, psychological benefits, many educators are emphatic also. They do not seem to have much use for its cultural effects, its stimulation to the mind of the growing youth, or its general disciplining qualities. On the other hand, they regard it as productive of narrowing results. Moreover, they see in it an undesirable . emphasis on military objects and procedure, and an inculcation of the idea that war is a necessary and inevitable guarantee of the security of countries.

Here are some typical opinions:

Military training "is undemocratic, barbaric and educationally wholly unwise."

John Dewey, distinguished educator and Professor of Philosophy, Columbia University.

"We do not want military training given to our schoolboys, because better bodies may be produced by proper physical training and directed school sports, and because these formative years should be devoted to the development of a spirit of internationalism which shall make war and preparation for war ultimately unnecessary."

Robert J. Aley, President (1916-17) of National Education Association; President of Butler College, Indianapolis.

"Against military training in our schools I have protested and would continue to protest, not because I object to the drill in itself (for I do not) but because I think we ought not to make that which implies a prepetuation of international hatreds and brutish warfare a purposeful feature of the education of our children."

John H. Finley, former State Commissioner of Education, New York, and now an editor of the "New York Times".

"All schools should provide such means of physical culture through outdoor games and exercises as will result in the best possible control of the body and all its members. I do not believe that military drill in our public schools is the best means to this end and I feel quite certain that rifle practice in the schools is undesirable. There is so much else that is better for all purposes that can be provided at much less cost."

Philander P. Claxton, former U. S. Commissioner of Education.

(Continued on page 18)

15

Universities and Colleges Where Military Training Is Compulsory

Military training was given last year in the following colleges and universities in the United States. Recent catalogs show that in the following 83 it is compulsory:

UNIVERSITIES

Col. of the City of New York
Cornell University
Creighton Univ., Omaha.
DePauw Univ., Greencastle, Ind.
Emory Univ., Georgia
Georgetown Univ., Washington, D. C., (Medical School)
Howard Univ., Wash., D. C.
Indiana Univ., Bloomington,
Lehigh University
Louisiana State Univ.
Municipal Univ. of Akron
New York University
Ohio State University
Pennsylvania State Col.
Purdue Univ., Lafayette, Ind.
State Univ. of Iowa
U. of Alabama
U. of Arizona
U. of Arkansas
U. of California
U. of Cincinnati
U. of Dayton, Dayton, O.
U. of Delaware
U. of Florida
U. of Georgia
U. of Idaho
U. of Illinois
U. of Kentucky
U. of Maine
U. of Maryland
U. of Minnesota
U. of Missouri
U. of Montana
U. of Nebraska
U. of Nevada
U. of New Hampshire
U. of North Carolina
U. of North Dakota
U. of Oklahoma
U. of Oregon
U. of South Dakota
U. of Tennessee
U. of Vermont
U. of Washington
U. of West Virginia
U. of Wyoming
Wilberforce Univ., Wilberforce, O.

AGRICULTURAL COLLEGES

Agr. and Mech. Col. of Texas
Agr. Col. of Utah
Alabama Polytechnic Inst.
Clemson Agr. Col., Clemson. S. C.
Colorado Agr. Col.
Connecticut Agr. Col.
Iowa State Col.
Kansas State Agr. Col.
Massachusetts Agr. Col.
Michigan Agr. Col.
Mississippi Agr. and Mech. Col.
Montana State Col. of Agr. and Mech. Arts
New Mexico Col. of Agr. and Mech. Arts
North Carolina State Col. of Agr. and Engineering
North Dakota Agr. Col.
North Georgia Agr. Col.
Oklahoma Agr. and Mech. Col.
Oregon Agr. Col.
Rhode Island State Col.
South Dakota State Col.
State Col. of Washington
Virginia Agr. and Mech. Col. and Polytechnic Institute

(Continued on next page)

COLLEGES AND TECHNICAL SCHOOLS

Boston Univ. (College of Business Administration)
California Institute of Technology
Coe Col., Cedar Rapids, Iowa
Col. of St. Thomas, St. Paul, Minn. (Preparatory Dept.)
Davidson Col., Davidson, N. C.
Drexel Institute, Philadelphia
Georgia School of Technology
Massachusetts Inst. of Tech.
Missouri State School of Mines
Presbyterian Col. of South Carolina, Clinton, S. C.
Rose Polytechnic Institute, Terre Haute, Ind.
Rutgers, New Brunswick, N. J.
State School of Mines, Golden, Colo.
Western Maryland

Universities and Colleges Where Military Training Is Elective

In these colleges and universities military training is elective:

UNIVERSITIES

Baylor, Dallas, Texas
Boston Univ. (College of Liberal Arts)
Denison, Granville, O.
Harvard
Johns Hopkins
Leland Stanford, Jr.
Northwestern Univ., Evanston, Ill.
Princeton
Syracuse
U. of Buffalo
U. of Chicago
U. of Kansas
U. of Michigan
U. of Pennsylvania
U. of Pittsburgh
U. of Porto Rico
U. of Utah
U. of Wisconsin
Washington, St. Louis
Western Reserve, Cleveland
Yale

COLLEGES AND TECHNICAL SCHOOLS

Albany Medical School
Campion Col., Prairie du Chien, Wis.
Carlisle School, Bamberg, S. C.
Carnegie Institute of Technology
Cornell Univ. Medical School New York City
Fairmount Col., Wichita, Kan.
George Washington Univ. Medical School
Gettysburg Col., Pa.
Jefferson Medical Col., Phila.
Knox, Galesburg, Ill.
Lafayette, Easton, Pa.
Little Rock Col., Arkansas
Loyola Col., Los Angeles
Medical Col., of Virginia, Richmond
North Pacific Col., of Oregon School of Dentistry, Portland
Northwestern Univ. Dental School, Evanston, Ill.
Ouachita Col., Arkadelphia, Ark.
Pomona Col., Claremont, Calif.
Ripon Col., Wisconsin
Rush Medical School, Chicago
St. John's, Annapolis
St. Louis Univ. School of Medicine
U. of California Medical School
U. of Oregon Medical School
Vanderbilt Univ. School of Medicine, Nashville
Western Kentucky State Normal School
Wofford Col., Spartanburg, S.C.

"Were the United States to become committed to military training for boys it would make her to appear more militaristic than any other great nation. To force military drill upon schoolboys would crowd out other and better forms of physical training. It would violate the best medical opinion. It would foster in young minds the idea that war is expected or necessary. It would present to the world the lamentable spectacle of the most democratic nation on earth doing what not one of the great military nations of Europe has done."

Samuel T. Dutton, Professor Emeritus of School Administration, Teachers College, Columbia University.

"I wonder if available evidence shows that military training does, in our American life, give better results in terms of obedience, discipline, precision, the sense of order and of obligation, than does non-military training. Are the graduates of our military schools better boys than those who come from other schools? As against that suggestion, I would put in evidence the statement that apparently the overwhelming majority of our schoolmasters have been opposed to military teaching."

Dr. Alexander Meiklejohn, former President of Amherst College.

COLLEGES SURRENDER CONTROL.

When an institution contracts with the War Department for the establishment of an R. O. T. C. unit it hands over to the Government control of this military instruction. Thus the R. O. T. C. courses, including the disposition of students' time for a specified number of hours per week, are made up in Washington. If the institution desires some variation from the standard program it must secure the approval of the Commander of the Corps Area in which it is situated. The Commander often resides hundreds of miles from the institution, so whether the recommended standard course is used or whether there is some variation, the whole thing is in the control not of the local college but of an outside agency powerfully organized about a special interest of its own. To let the camel of militarism thus get his nose under the tent of academic independence seems a dangerous experiment. One is not sure how seductive the military money may prove which builds a handsome armory, which pays for part of the faculty, and which subsidizes students.

College presidents when they sign up with the Government for the R. O. T. C. specifically promise, among other things, "to use their endeavors to promote and further the objects for which the training corps is organized." Students at the Michigan State College of Agriculture are informed: "Only the Professor of Military Science and Training has authority to excuse and no other excuse is valid." The University of California, in a circular issued in August, 1924, asserts that students who register and do not attend classes in military subjects will be dismissed

18

from the University. Those institutions whose military training and morale is most approved by the War Department are singled out for distinguished rating. In the competition to become a "distinguished college" faculty members will sometimes give the military interests priority over other work. The deans of two colleges in an Eastern university not long ago required professors and instructors in their colleges to excuse undergraduates from regular recitations and lectures in order that a military inspection might be carried through. The notice to their faculty colleagues said, "It is a fact that the consequences of our recognition by the War Department as a 'distinguished college' may be of real importance to the institution. On this account the administration is conceding this extraordinary request." *

A New Note in the Catalogs

In many catalogs occur glowing passages designed, apparently, to "sell" military training to prospective students. Some of these passages are changed only slightly, or quoted verbatim, from publications of the War Department. Indeed, the phraseology and educational philosophy current on many a campus in this country today are borrowed from majors and colonels in Washington. "Every college man should be taught the meaning of discipline, the power of confidence, the value of self-control, the requisites of leadership, respect for authority, the force of morale, the care of mind and body, and the rewards of promptness and obedience," runs the catalog of Georgetown University, in much the style of an army recruiting officer. "The primary purpose of the R. O. T. C. is to provide systematic military training at civil educational institutions for the purpose of qualifying selected students of such institutions for appointment as reserve officers in the military forces of the United States"—so read the catalogs of Rose Polytechnic Institute at Terre Haute, Ind., of Davidson College at Davidson, N. C., of the University of Montana at Missoula, and of other colleges—and so, word for word, reads paragraph two of Section 1 of Army Regulations No. 145-10. Of the catalogs examined for this pamphlet the fact that the passage was not original with the writer has been indicated in only one.

---

* Memorandum of April 26, 1925, signed by Dean of College of Arts and Pure Science and Dean of College of Engineering, New York University.

WHERE MILITARY TRAINING IS COMPULSORY.

It is impossible, without exhaustive search, to give a complete list of schools and colleges in which military training is compulsory. But the number is large, especially of colleges. An examination of the catalogs of 121 of the 124 colleges and universities having units of the R. O. T. C. showed that in 83 of these institutions military training is compulsory for the students in one or more departments of the school.* Some schools exclude the department of law, or the department of dentistry, or of pharmacy, or one or more other departments, from the compulsory requirement. In schools where military training is compulsory, the requirement usually applies to the first two years of the student's education; after that he may continue or not, as he chooses. In one school the reqirement applies to the whole four years, and in a few schools to only one year. On pages 16-17 is given a list of colleges and universities in which, as revealed by this study of catalogs, military training is required of all male students who are not physically disqualified and who are not "aliens". On page 2 is given a list of cities in which there are high schools with compulsory, as well as high schools with elective, military training.

FALLACY THAT A COLLEGE MUST MAINTAIN COMPULSORY MILITARY TRAINING.

A fallacy in regard to compulsion should be cleared up. The Federal Government does not officially require any school to make the military training that it offers compulsory on individual students. If a school or college makes military training compulsory, it is doing so under its own responsibility, so far as the United States government is concerned; some few state legislatures have passed laws requiring that military training be made compulsory at some schools within those states, but that is all. No branch or department of the Federal Government requires that military training be compulsory; not even land grant colleges —though the contrary is often asserted—are under any obligation to make training compulsory. The situation is this:

The Morrill Land Grant Act, about which something has been said earlier, gave land to the states on condition that the land be sold, the proceeds invested and the income derived therefrom used for the "maintenance of at least one college where the object shall be, without excluding other scientific and classical studies,

---

*The writer wishes to thank Miss Inez Cavert for valuable assistance in compiling this information.

and *including military tactics,* to teach such branches of learning as are related to agriculture and the mechanic arts, in such manner as the legislatures of the states may respectively prescribe, in order to promote the liberal and practical education of the industrial classes in the several pursuits and professions in life." (Italics ours). Most states in the Union accepted the benefits of this act and established land-grant colleges. A number of state universities are such colleges.

There is, however, nothing in this act that requires a college to maintain a *compulsory* course in military tactics. *The college must offer a course, but it may leave it to its students whether they take the course or not;* in other words, the course may be elective. Authorities have rendered decisions on this point again and again. In July, 1923, the question was submitted to the Commissioner of the Interior by the War Department itself, protesting against the action of the University of Wisconsin, a land grant college, in changing its instruction in military tactics from compulsory to elective courses. The Commissioner of the Interior, who passes upon reports from land grant colleges showing whether they are living up to the requirements of the Morrill Act, said in his opinion:

" . . . According to the Act approved July 2nd, 1862, (the Morrill Land Grant Act), it is clear that the branches of instruction, which include military tactics, are to be taught 'in such manner as the legislatures of the States may respectfully prescribe' . . .

"Military training according to the Federal law is clearly placed in the same category as the other branches of learning which are named. Instruction in Military tactics is obviously a requirement on the states as are the other branches which are mentioned. It does not appear, however, from the Federal legislation that instruction in military tactics is any more obligatory on the individual student than is instruction in agriculture or mechanic arts. The common practice of excepting third and fourth year students as well as many first and second year students for various reasons seems to be a recognition of the principle just stated."

So also the National Defense Act, under which most of the military training which we have been discussing has been established, does not require any school to maintain a compulsory form of military education. Under date of November 18, 1924, Secretary of War Weeks wrote to Walter C. Longstreth, a lawyer of Philadelphia, who had directed an inquiry to him:

"I am pleased to inform you that the National Defense Act

21

does not make military training compulsory at any of the institutions which receive the benefits authorized by the Act. *"So far as the War Department is concerned it is optional with the authorities of the school, college or university whether military training shall be an elective or a compulsory course in the curriculum."* (Italics ours.)*

Colleges and other schools establishing units of the R.O.T.C. fill out application blanks supplied by the War Department. This application recites that the school in question agrees "to establish and maintain a two years' compulsory (or elective) course of military training."* The college or school is free to choose whether it will strike out the words in parentheses, and so agree to maintain a compulsory course in military training, or whether it will strike out the word "compulsory" and so agree to maintain an elective course. Whichever it does, *the act is its own.*

How Colleges Enforce Compulsion.

Although there is thus no compulsion to maintain compulsory courses, many schools and colleges make their courses compulsory, and it sometimes goes hard with the young man who refuses the yoke. Robert Dieffenbacher at Pennsylvania State College, desiring to be relieved of his uniform and to discontinue military training, petitioned the university officials to that effect. They refused to allow him to be excused; indeed, did not the college catalog declare that "every male student of the Freshman, Sophomore and special classes is required to enroll for military instruction unless he is physically disqualified". Mr. Dieffenbacher was male and physically qualified, but he happened to have a conscience which objected to military pursiuts, so he decided that he would have to leave the college of his choice and pursue his education elsewhere. At last reports he was duly enrolled at Lafayette College, where military training is offered but not required.

But the story does not end there. At the time when young Dieffenbacher got into trouble, Frank I. Olmstead, the secretary

---

*From a letter to Walter C. Longstreth, quoted in a pamphlet entitled "Regarding Military Training at Universities", 1925, prepared for the Peace and Service Committee of the Philadelphia Yearly Meeting of Friends, 1305 Arch St., Phila. Pa.

*The National Defense Act declares that schools taking advantage of War Department assistance in establishing R. O. T. C. units must agree to maintain "a two years' *elective or compulsory* course". In framing its application blank, the War Department reversed the order of these important words.

22

of the student branch of the Y. M. C. A. at Penn State, invited speakers to address the Y. M. C. A. Forum on both sides of the question of compulsory training. He relates what happened in a letter:

"Our Y. M. C. A. had both sides of the case presented in our Forum, and offered to print letters on both sides in the Penn State Y. M. C. A. Alumni News-Letter. Shortly thereafter, I was called into the office of the college President, and requested not to mention the Dieffenbacher case again in speech or print. I appealed to our Board of Directors, who sustained the President in his request. I resigned as a protest against this infringement of free speech and press, and to sustain the principle of the right of the Young Men's Christian Association to seek Christian truth."

Many people have heard what happened to Miss Henrietta Perkins, editor of the *Beanpot,* a comic magazine published by the students of Boston University, when she boldly ventured to devote a number of that magazine to the R. O. T. C. In Miss Perkins' magazine appeared much humorous and some serious ridicule of the R. O. T. C. and of the military aroma that it exhaled around the Boston University campus. Miss Perkins was sharply reprimanded and deprived of her editorial mantle. She was summarily removed from the board of the *Beanpot,* and only grudgingly allowed to continue as a student of the University. The entire number of the offending periodical was suppressed.

GROUPS OF STUDENTS, HERE AND THERE, ARE PROTESTING.

Sturdy protests by students occur here and there. At the University of Minnesota an *Anti-Compulsory Military Drill League* has been formed, and has issued a printed "indictment" of compulsory training. It has assisted in holding mass meetings among students to bring out the full strength of the opposition to military coercion and it has circulated petitions, not only among students, but among members of the faculty, state legislators and citizens generally, in order to create sufficient protest against compulsory training to persuade the Board of Regents to make the training optional. Whether it will succeed, it is now too early to tell.

At the University of Wisconsin students sharply criticized the compulsory nature of military training three years ago and the university administration decided to make military training elective. An act of the state legislature of Wisconsin now requires that such training be elective. Pomona College, California, now has elective military training following a period of compulsory training.

Student objection to military training has been given strong

23

voice at the Universities of California, Kansas, Missouri, Nebraska and Georgia, and also at Syracuse University, Pennsylvania State College, Boston University, College of the City of New York and other colleges. It is growing, and the prospect is that it may become an effective factor in determining policy at a number of institutions.

Students at the University of Washington in Seattle presented a petition to their Board of Regents in May, 1925, asking that military training be optional. This read in part:

"We, the undersigned, believing that University students should not be compelled to study military science, respectfully request the authorities of the University to make this study OPTIONAL. The reasons for this request are briefly stated as follows:

1. Any system of enforced military drill is repugnant to many Americans, and is contrary to American principles of freedom and democracy.

2. Young men outside of college are not obliged to take part in army life; neither should students be forced into military service against their will.

3. It cannot be expected that students should study military science in order to repay the state for the opportunity to get a higher education, for leading thinkers have always held that an enlightened population is in itself one of the chief assets of a state and constitutes the principal factor of its safety.

4. Many students, from religious motives, object to the theory of warfare and hold that the study of military science has a brutalizing effect upon individuals. These students should be permitted to choose gymnasium work instead of military science.

5. As to the plan of national defense outlined by army men we feel that their program of preparedness, far from adding to the security of our country, is certain to induce warfare since it arouses irritation, suspicion and fear among other nations, postpones the day of international disarmament, and opens the door to continued corruption and profiteering out of which munition manufacturers and contractors for army supplies will reap untold profits.

6. War should be outlawed. So long as thousands of school boys are forced, hoaxed or bribed into military service it will be impossible to abolish the institution."

SUBSIDIZING THE STUDENT.

But even if compulsion were to go—and it is at present increasing, not lessening—there would still be the factor of War Department propaganda. Backed by an annual appropriation, such as the $3,818,020 given by Congress for R. O. T. C. expenses in 1925, the military officials are able to make money talk to students. Under the terms of the National Defense Act students in the junior division and those taking the basic course in the senior division receive uniforms to wear while they are undergoing training. Those in the basic course receive, also, travel allowance to and from a summer camp, if they elect to attend one; they receive subsistence while there. Students in the advanced course of the senior division receive more. They get not only uniforms but a subsidy in cash. They are given "commutation of subsistence," which is in reality money toward their living expenses. This payment is issued to them at the rate of thirty cents a day for 312 days, and thus amounts to $93.60 for each year, or $187.20 for the two years —a sum sufficient to help many a poor lad through school. In addition while in camp they receive wages at the lowest rate of Regular Army pay, or seventy cents a day. This adds $29.40 to their receipts, bringing the total in actual cash up to $216.60.

The college catalogs hold out the Government's lure. At the University of Delaware it is announced that each student may expect to get $250 above expenses; at Colorado Agricultural College, between $200 and $300; at Leland Stanford and the Colorado School of Mines, $9 a month; at Western Maryland College "over $200 in cash"; at North Georgia Agricultural College "about $170"; and at George Washington University $110 to $150. So it goes. To a poor boy struggling to get an education these sums are important.

Overcoats "Suitable for Civilian Wear"

And money is not the only attraction. The twelve students highest in rifle marksmanship, according to the catalog of Georgetown University, are organized into an R. O. T. C. rifle team and given the privilege of a four weeks' trip to the National rifle matches. At Colorado Agricultural College students are reminded that polo horses are furnished by the War Department and that the R. O. T. C. polo team is sent to the Interstate College Polo Tournament, while the R. O. T. C. band accompanies the football team on two out-of-town trips. Moreover, the college provides an "overcoat suitable for wear with both uniforms and civilian clothing"; winters are sharp in Colorado. The work of the cavalry corps at the University of Arizona is described as consisting largely of riding school work, cross country riding, exhibition and horse show riding, polo, cavalry marches, and care and treatment of animals. "Regular horse shows are held," reads the catalogue, "and a polo club competes with several nearby cavalry regimental teams." What young lad wouldn't be tempted to military training by such inducements as these?

The Medal, the Sabre and the Military Ball

Besides there are medals and other awards. A sabre and scabbard are given each year to every student who completes the military course satisfactorily at Oklahoma Agricultural College. The University of Maryland bestows a military medal and a silver mounted sword each year upon the captain of the best drilled company. At the University of Arizona a sabre is given annually to the "most efficient commissioned cadet officer." It is a "Pershing medal" that is presented to the most efficient soldier at the University of Nebraska. Rutgers College encourages the military spirit by inscribing, on a tablet in the gymnasium, the name of the "best soldier" each year. Military prizes are awarded annually at the University of Illinois, the University of Wisconsin and the North Georgia Agricultural College. To festivities such as the "Junior Hop" and the "Senior Prom" the University of Wisconsin has added a "military ball," to which the girls of the university and the men and women of Madison come in greater or smaller numbers. Many colleges have similar dances. At Nebraska the whole student body annually elects the most popular girl in college as "honorary colonel." Military fraternities have grown in strength. *Scabbard and Blade,* one of these, organized at a land-grant college in 1905, now has chapters in fifty-three colleges and universities. The regular Greek letter fraternities not infrequently compete among themselves to get the greatest number of officers as members.

"Selling" Military Training.

Too often all these inducements are played up for "selling" military training to the prospective student, as reported by students here and there. "You get a tailor made uniform which saves your regular suit. The pay is better than you can get elsewhere for the amount of work. The college gives you credit too. There's a lot of honor in it for you." Parades and public exhibitions "give you training in managing men." "Of course the first two years are hard but when you get to be an officer you will think it worth while. Don't kick about things you don't like or don't understand, just boost!"

While some of these appeals—which play up the monetary or scholastic rewards, or flatter the egotism of the prospective young officer, or stress the necessity for unthinking mass action —have at times a humorous side, there is also a deeper aspect which is tragic.

How Such Inducements Work.

The writer has knowledge of more than one immature boy who was led on by such blandishments to elect military training and to enter into obligations with his school, or the Government, which he later realized did not involve just "boosting the school" but committing himself to an alignment with the world's forces of militarism—forces which he now regards as questionable or evil. In such a situation the boy's inner sense of duty is torn between loyalty to his contract, an obligation felt toward his parents to go on and get his college degree and, on the other hand, loyalty to his conscience, to the insistent voice of his youth calling him to throw his full strength into the crucial moral battle of his generation, the battle to rid this world of war. It must needs be, perhaps, that in the complicated obligations of human life such oppositions of duty will occur, but woe to the man or the institution that leads youth into them by misrepresentations of truth.

Fomenting Distrust of Other Nations.

More sinister than such boosting talks as these is the nurturing of distrust toward other nations. In conversations between military instructors and students, in class-rooms of the R. O. T. C., and on other occasions brought about by military training, particular nations are singled out for mention and the attitude is glorified. We do not suggest that this is done with the approval of the War Department, or that officials in Washington would sanction it. But the individual military instructor is evidently under a temptation that he cannot resist. "Look out for Japan! Look out for Great Britian! Beware of Germany!" say these instructors to their students, and the distrust grows. We have the testimony of many students that such things go on. "The United States is getting the dirty end of the stick in the 5-5-3 ratio", has said more than one officer giving military instruction, in commenting upon the naval disarmament program approved by the Washington Conference. "War is natural, war is human, war is inevitable, war is right", run their remarks. They bid their listeners to be prepared to defend their country and "Be Prepared!" is the slogan to which the walls in many classrooms have echoed since the rise of the R. O. T. C.

One straight speaking army officer has cried out against the whole miserable business:

"Good citizenship." he says, "is an excellent thing, and so are religion, filial affection and brotherly love. But they are not the ends of an army. An army exists to kill men, when ordered, in the nation's quarrel, irrespective of justice. It should train its men to that single end. . . . If we object to any of our citizens thus specializing on murderous and unchristian activities, we should abolish the army. If we want an army, we should recognize it for what it is. We should not lie about its being a school for citizenship or manual training, nor clutter up its drill grounds with disciples for these irrelevant arts."*

THE IMPORTANT ISSUES.

When we come now to summarize the dangers created by the push for military training in our schools, there stand out certain issues which are the ones this pamphlet has sought to make clear

FIRST: Such military training as we have been discussing is dangerous *because of its extent and the determination of the War Department to stimulate its further growth.*

In 1915 there were no summer camps, no R. O. T. C., only 119 officers detailed to military schools; in 1920 we have a National Defense Act legalizing a military drive upon civil institutions; in 1925 Congress appropriates more than $5,900,000 for schools and camps combined, the War Department assigns 768 officers and 1,064 enlisted men to carry on training and at least 160,000 young Americans come under direct army influence in this way. This is 15,000 more than the total membership of our active army including reserves on active duty. In 1914 the United States had a regular army of but 92,482‡ recruited without any R. O. T. C. and C. M. T. C. at all.

Such figures speak for themselves and yet they do not tell the whole story for *it is planned to draw out of the R. O. T. C. and C. M. T. C. a large officer class which could organize man power reserves from the nation.* The Adjutant General of the Army figures that the unorganized man power reserves of the country are 16.792,781.† Here is the danger of military bureaucracy— that we should allow to grow up in this country the Frankenstein of a professional war thinking, war planning, war glorifying class, and that we should feed it the flower of American youth.

The evil of such a policy would reach out to stimulate other

---

* "The American Mercury", June, 1925. Article, "The Uplift Hits the Army", by an Army Officer, pp. 136-141. Reprinted in Army and Navy Register, July 25, 1925.

‡ New International Yearbook for 1914, p. 720.

† Table by Adjutant General U. S. Army, *World Almanac*, 1925, p. 241.

countries, through fear, to build up competitive military training for their youth reserves. It is the sense of power to lord things over smaller nations that has developed militarism in its most dangerous forms. And both with regard to the interactions of a state among other states and the balance of military to civilian population within a state's own bounds, all history shows that when military establishments attain a certain size, somewhere a saturation danger point is reached; and the nations especially which need most to beware of it, are those which are tempted by their strength.

SECOND: In line with this danger is the issue raised by *making training compulsory in eighty-three American colleges and many public schools.* Students all over the country feel this is abrogating the rights of conscience. They are saying that enforced military drill is contrary to American principles and contrary to the ideals of the stalwart men who founded our country. In 'Europe we have seen how conscription is the all reaching arm by which militarism brings the manhood of the nations to its maw; until it is abolished no real disarmament or security can come. But compulsory drill in schools and colleges enforced by academic authorities is only one step this side of universal military service enforced on pain of imprisonment by the state.

Indeed, it is reported that the Joint Board of the Army and Navy has already prepared and will cause to be introduced into the next Congress a bill giving the President power to conscript all males between the ages of 18 and 30 into the military service of the United States when Congress shall declare that a national emergency exists.* For conscientious objectors it provides that the President may order them into what he decides is non-combatant service. But the provision is such that should any question arise as to whether certain service really is non-combatant, or whether the state has a right to conscript personal work in any form, it will be *the President's conscience which decides these things for others, and not a man's conscience deciding for himself.*

Never yet has progress come by institutions putting such ban on individual dissent. New truth for mankind, new social advance, is perceived and acted on first by lone individuals and small groups, and never, in the beginning, by majorities or institutions. When they crush inconvenient dissent they crush also their own chance of growth. For twenty-five centuries, from Socrates on, by trial and error, at great cost and pain, the proof

---

* *New York Times, Sept.* 24, 1925.

has accumulated that social interest is served by the man who reverences conscience as his King. By all her best traditions America ought to stand for this and her colleges foster individual initiative and freedom in the breasts of all her sons.

THIRD: Allied to moral freedom for the individual is *the question of freedom of teaching for the Universities themselves.* We do not say that, as yet, the War Department interferes with civilian teaching but there is evident danger that it may if the present partnership between it and our educational institutions is not dissolved. He who pays for the piper generally picks the tune so that when universities encourage military interests to build armories on their campuses, to appoint and pay for military professors on their faculties, to give subsidies to students who take military courses, and when finally they hand over to the U. S. War Department complete control of all military instruction, a precedent is set whose possible consequences to academic freedom should be clearly foreseen. If, let us say, a professor of history giving revisionist views on guilt for the war, or a Y. M. C. A. secretary keeping his forum open to speakers who oppose "preparedness", should come into clash with the Department of Military Science and Tactics and if their dispute should wax warm, would the President of the University keep open the channels of free discussion impartially for both sides? He might, but cases have occurred where he did not*, and it is easy to see how the pressure of military money and organization could lead him to conclude that the "best interests of the university" demanded silence from the history professor, or no more "preparedness" discussions at the "Y". It would be serious indeed if while waging the fight for academic freedom against religious sectarianism and big business trusteeship our colleges should have to encounter also a military lobby and machine.

FOURTH: Military training raises the issue of an *educational tendency towards a psychology for war or peace.* For, even without charging that it produces *desire* for war or glory, it is hardly to be questioned that it makes for a *mind-set* which automatically thinks of war as the ultimate "sanction" to be used by patriotism, the one process which in some circumstances national honor and necessity must employ. And it is precisely such commonly held assumptions that stand in the way of disarmament and of creating faith in a League of Nations and World Court such as could really be trusted to work out peace processes for the settlement of all international strife.

---

* Pennsylvania State College—op. cit. p. 22. 23.

The world's success or failure in this matter of solving conflict by processes of peace instead of war seems largely to hinge upon the courage of its faith plus a fresh intellectual and spiritual approach to the problem. The schools and colleges of today should give predominant emphasis to this; but can they, when admitting the Department of War to such prominence as many do? The deep danger of military training is not that it teaches a boy how to handle a rifle, but that it leads him to *think* in the *psychology of war.*

FINALLY: *What then shall we do?* In a number of institutions student groups have already started a movement against compulsion. Similarly fathers and mothers with children in high schools where there is drill can protest to school boards, and by writing to local newspapers, etc., start their communities discussing the advantages and disadvantages of high school military training. Parent—teacher associations, women's clubs, labor groups, community forums and other organizations can get speakers to address meetings; appropriate resolutions can be adopted and sent out. Young people's classes in Sunday schools can debate the question from the standpoint of what Christian idealism would require Trustees of denominational colleges, and of those serving Christian constituencies, should be made to face the implications of a supposedly Christian institution maintaining an official teaching partnership with a nationalist Department of War. *Each local school, each local college and university has the power and right not to maintain compulsory military training; it has also the right—if it be not a land grant college—not to have any military training at all.* The immediate points therefore at which this training can be opposed are the educational authorities of the institutions where it is given. Citizens who are against it may also send protests to their representatives in Congress. (In some cases State Legislatures also.) The House and Senate at Washington pass each year the appropriation bill for army expenses. When taxpayers throughout the country demand that no more taxes shall be used to subsidize military training in civil educational institutions, Congress can stop it; and America will then go back in this matter to the position she has safely and honorably held through all her history down to the tragic days of the great European war.

Your co-operation is solicited in supporting the action suggested in the foreword to this pamphlet. A committee has been formed to urge nation-wide consideration of this question. Will you help by sending us further information concerning the campaign for or against military training in your locality?

Additional copies of this pamphlet may be obtained at the rate of 10 cents each; $1.00 for 15; $5.00 per hundred; $45.00 per thousand, postpaid, from

COMMITTEE ON MILITARY TRAINING

387 Bible House, Astor Place,
New York City.

Universal Military Training
Our Latest Cure-All

By OSWALD GARRISON VILLARD

Editor of the *New York Nation*

I

IN the years to come, none of the recent amazing phenomena will, I am sure, cause greater wonderment than our latest discovery that universal military service is the cure-all for every one of our American ills. Do we wish to defend our country? We have but to adopt the system of training every boy to be a soldier, and the problem is solved. Do we wish to become industrially efficient? Then let us forget all about vocational training, but give every American a year under arms, and presto! we shall outdo Germany in scientific efficiency and management. Is our youth lawless and undisciplined? Universal compulsory service will end that once for all. Is our democracy halting? It is the tonic of a democratic army that we need in which all men shall pay for the privileges of citizenship by a year of preparation for poison gas and of learning how to destroy other human beings. Our melting-pot is a failure? Then let us pour into it the iron of militarism, and it will fuse every element at once. Finally, if we need an American soul—and the war has suddenly taught us that this glorious country lacks a soul! —it is the remedy of universal military service that is to supply our spiritual needs and give us the ability to feel as one, to think as one, to steer towards our destiny as of one mind, imperialistically.

It is so alluring and so entrancingly easy, the wonder is that we have never thought of it before. We saw it going on in France and Germany and Russia, but it seemed altogether repulsive in its forms. Americans to be conscripted? Heaven forbid. There rose before us the unutterable cruelties of non-commissioned officers and even of the officers—visions of the thousands of men coming to our shores with hands mutilated to avoid the barracks with their open immoralities, their bitter hardships, the loss of three years of so many working lives. The "Red Rosa," Rosa Luxembourg, with her 10,000 authenticated instances of cruelties to German soldiers, inflicted by their own countrymen behind the screen of official authority, explained to us why so many young Germans emigrated

(1)

before becoming of military age. In speaking of the case of one
soldier horribly abused at Metz, the "Red Rosa" declared: "It is
certainly one of those dramas which are enacted day in and day out
in German barracks, although the groans of the actors never reach
our ears." When the German army sought to prosecute her it was
announced that she would call 1,030 eye-witnesses to grievous
abuses of military authority in Germany's "democratic" army, but
she went to jail none the less.

II

In Germany, of course, universal service is not in the least democratic, save that all must serve. Upon that we can surely all agree.
The autocracy rules the army, and the aristocracy is fortressed by
it. More than one debate in the Reichstag has been enlivened by
the bitter attacks by bourgeois orators against the favoritism
shown to the Imperial Guards and to other fashionable regiments.
There is even a caste within a caste, for men who pass through the
gymnasia need serve but one year. Those whose fathers are too
poor to educate them thus must give two years of their lives to
carrying arms. The spirit of arrogance and aristocracy which the
military life, with its dueling, its mediaeval code of honor, fosters,
is about as anti-democratic as anything in the world. When men,
merely by reason of the coat they wear, deem themselves sacrosanct
and especially privileged, even to the extent of running through
civilians by whom they fancy themselves insulted, or of preparing
to turn their machine-guns upon their civilian fellow-townsmen,
as in Zabern, it is obviously absurd to contend that the system of
which they are the products smacks, save in the remotest, of anything democratic.*

And never, save in Russia, was there a better illustration of the
truth of our own James Madison's saying that "large armies and
heavy taxes are the best-known instruments for bringing the many
under the dominion of the few." General von Falkenhayn, Chief of
Staff and War Minister, was not altogether far from the truth
when he said that **but for the army "not a stone of the Reichstag
building would remain in place,"** provided we assume that he meant
to typify by the Reichstag building the present form of government
in Berlin. No one need look further than the Russian system of

universal service for a complete reason for the failure of the first Russian revolution of this century. **The truth is that men of noble spirit are in every land crushed by the whole system of compulsory military labor precisely as compulsory servitude deadens men's souls everywhere.**

And those Americans who see in the French army a perfect model for ourselves would do well to forget neither the shocking revelations of graft which have come to light before and since the war, nor the depths of infamy sounded by the military in the Dreyfus case, nor the fact that General Boulanger came within an ace of upsetting the Republic he had taken oath to preserve.* But, we are told, Australia is democratic, quite like ourselves, and Australia has dedicated its youth to a training in arms with much resultant good in the present campaign. Why should we not be like Australia? Surely, there is no militarism there. And look at Switzerland! Does it not point the way? Well, so far as the latter is concerned, it does not. There is no comparison whatever between a little homogeneous country of about four millions— homogeneous despite the use of three languages—with a small and extremely mountainous country to defend, and our own vast continent.

But in one respect, the Swiss system does set an admirable example to the United States: It allows no general to exist save after the declaration of war. Its highest officer is a colonel. No major-generals parade the country urging "preparedness"; no brigadiers bewail the terrible fate that will overtake Switzerland if her standing force is not doubled at once. Yet even in Switzerland, if report be true, there is an anti-army party, people who complain that the military business has become ominous ever since so many of the younger officers have been serving in the German army and become imbued with the spirit of the Prussian General Staff, just as, according to a prominent Australian, speaking in a public meeting in London a few months ago, the feeling against conscription of boys was so intense in Australia that the law compelling this servitude would have been repealed had not the war come just when it did. Perhaps the fact that in fifteen years some 22,000 Australian boys have been punished for refusal to perform military service, or for minor infractions of discipline, a large proportion by jail sentences, may have had something to do with the growing feeling against it. As to its merits, there is as much difference of military

*January, 1889.

opinion in regard to its work, as it to be found in regard to the value of our own military forces.

III

But let us grant for the sake of argument that there is solid worth in the Australian and Swiss systems, and less militaristic danger than under any other. Would the same hold true with us? Australia is but a colony, unable to make war by itself, controlled and protected by the power of the mother country's fleet. Switzerland, by her geographical and ethnic situation and the scarcity of her numbers, cannot dream of wars of conquest. She is not a world power. She has no colonies, or overseas entanglements, or foreign alliances. How different is our situation! **We have powerful military cliques, great aggregations of capital seeking outlet abroad and engineered by the same groups of privileged citizens who have been behind the Six-Power Chinese loan, who desire to exploit the Philippines for our own benefit, who have set up in Nicaragua a government upheld to-day only by American bayonets, who desire commercially to conquer the remainder of the hemisphere. We have seen outbursts of jingo passion in 1849 and 1898 marked by the stealing of other people's lands. The universal arming of the nation —what would it not mean in another such period of excitement under the rule of conscienceless and time-serving legislators, or administrators, or by generals gone into politics, with eyes keen only for a nation's aggrandizement and viewing every question from the standpoint of a soldier!**

History shows us clearly what it all might mean. Leaving aside the fate of the ancient republics, should we not recall what happened to the new-born French Republic? The nation rushed to arms, and out of the hurly-burly emerged the imperial figure which became the scourge of Europe. Such was the sudden transformation of a nation that but a few years before was imbued with the spirit of liberty, fraternity, and equality, whose doctrine did permeate all Europe to its very lasting betterment. But this tide of good-will, this spirit of universal brotherhood, was conquered by the militaristic spirit and militarism until it became, not the great leavening, leveling influence it should have become, but a menace for all the world against which all the nations of Europe were compelled to unite. Now we Americans, of course, think that nothing of the kind can happen to us—that we merely seek peace and to defend our own. Is it utterly without significance that our most distinguished Rear Admiral goes up and down the country preaching that the American flag shall be carried at once to Cape Horn; that every republic to the south of us shall be conquered? Does it mean nothing that the Navy League demands that we shall take what they call "our rightful share of oversea trade" and seize upon land which has not already been preëmpted by other strong nations for colonies for the United States? It is not true that we are already extending our government over the Caribbean by force of bayonets?

We have one hundred millions of people; we have neighbors on our borders whom we could easily crush if we chose. To the south of us a score of republics fear every military move we make. It is an historic fact that even before the war in Europe the menace of our rapidly growing fleet was urged in the Reichstag, in the British and Japanese Parliaments, as the reason for further increase of their naval armaments. **Any introduction of universal military servitude in the Western world would send a chill over the entire American continent and be viewed with alarm by the rest of the world.**

IV

Assuming that we are going to think of nobody else, and to blind our eyes to the obvious effects abroad of our arming—what does universal service mean? If it is to be for one year, fully seven hundred thousand young men will be annually withdrawn from productive labor; if it is to be for two years, and on the German model, our standing army would be at least a million four hundred thousand, or nearly double that of Germany, in 1914. It would mean so vast a machinery of control and discipline that no other department could compare with it in expense or in the multitude of its permanent employes. Has any one in America who is advocating universal service yet computed the cost, direct or indirect, to the nation? If so, I have not seen it.* Even on the dilettante Swiss and Australian basis, it would be stupendous. If carried out under federal supervision, it would enormously increase our most favored class of citizens—our military and naval servants—and their pension rolls. Abroad the conscripts receive only a few cents a day for their service, which is practically unpaid (in Turkey, even in war time, the soldier gets but twenty-five cents a month). Would

*The utter indifference to the element of cost, both as to actual budget cost and the even more serious item of the economic waste involved, on the part of the advocates of universal military training was well exemplified during the debate in the Senate in March, 1918, when the spokesmen for compulsory training freely admitted that they had no data as to probable expense but contended that the expense did not matter. Here, apparently, is to be one branch of the government which is to be given a blank check on the Treasury, not in times of war merely, but in times of peace.—*Note by A. U. A. M.*

our American youth stand for this when our National Guard has just now, by skilful political influence, succeeded in getting itself on the federal pay-roll—the first time that men have been so paid, yet remained important political factors in civil life? But we need have less concern with the financial cost and the creation of a dangerous military caste and the terrible burden of taxation than with the indirect results.

For what those do not see who feel that universal service is what we need to make patriots by the million is that the spirit of universal servitude, whether Australian, German, or Swiss, makes directly against the American ideal, for it inculcates blind obedience to the will of others, subordination to those who are masters, not necessarily because of superior wisdom or fitness, but largely because of accident. Heretofore we have always valued the American's self-assertiveness—yes, his refusal to recognize masters, his independence of thought and action, his mental alertness, particularly the happy-go-lucky Yankee initiative and individuality, as some of his best characteristics. We hated the servile obedience of the foreigner. Indeed, our whole American experiment was founded as a protest against certain tendencies abroad akin to those we are now asked to make dominant by means of universal service. The manhood of our western pioneers, the daring spirit of those who conquered the wildernesses were our admiration. They might verge on the lawless at times, but militarism gave them nothing and could add nothing to their virile courage and their ability to take care of themselves. Now we are to prefer all men cast in one mould, drilled into one way of thinking, and taught blind obedience to those set above them. Formerly, we deemed it most worth while that all men should have their own opinions, express them freely, and if their consciences dictated, differ with their rulers if they saw fit. The principle of voluntary military service is directly connected with the principle of freedom of conscience which led to the foundation of Massachusetts and of Pennsylvania. Universal conscription, however disguised, by whatever foreign name it is characterized, makes against freedom of conscience and drives men into intellectual slavery.

Take the education of our boys. Recently, at a joint meeting of two schoolmasters' associations, there were divided views on some issues, but none apparently as to the utter lawlessness of our American youth and the complete failure of our private schools to reduce them to subordination by means of mental and moral discipline. And so there were many who grasped with joy at the universal military-drill idea to retrieve for them the ground lost by their own failure to do the fundamental thing they pledged themselves to accomplish. Of course, they knew little or nothing about universal service; perhaps it was the unexplored mystery of it that appealed. Many Americans are quite sure that the latest untried remedy, be it some law, or the initiative and referendum, or the recall of judicial decisions, or some other panacea, is, by reason of its very newness, just the medicine for a given ill they have been looking for. So with these school teachers. Ignoring the fact that our private military schools have been anything but popular, and, only in exceptional cases, of high standing, they turn to military drill as to a last straw. But some of them do not even stop there; they want everybody subjected to military service. They forget that to some of their boys enforced military training may be as poison, and do not inquire whether they are not suddenly exalting the physical above the intellectual. The only thing that stands out about it is that they, too, confessing themselves and their judgment failures heretofore, are now ready to take a leap into the dark.

V

Advocates of military preparedness are fond of likening their policies to the insurance policy upon our edifices. But there is a point beyond which no man would increase his premiums upon any given premises; he would tear them down to get a lower rate on a more modern structure, or he would build a concrete structure and do away with insurance altogether. So the price of universal military servitude is far too great a price to pay for insuring peace by any free peoples. Its dangers, its contaminating effects, **the terrible weapon it forges for rulers,** its reducing men to a dead level, far offset the alleged advantages of physical betterment, greater practical efficiency and energy, and a sense of responsibility to the nation. For all of these things the price of compulsory service would be too heavy. For it does not train the unfit or build up the weak, and it is not meant or intended to increase efficiency in civil life. Its primary purpose is to turn out killers, not workers. It often destroys those it would benefit—no less than ten thousand three hundred German conscripts have committed suicide in the last thirty years, or at the rate of one a day. There was a time when the price of social order was that human beings should go armed all the time, when they lived and ate and slept with their weapons by their sides. Humanity was deemed to have advanced itself from this stage until the present time has seen a return to it in the conscript armies of Europe. **Surely, if the price of each man's carrying arms against another was too great to pay, the social cost of arming every man in a nation against all the men of other nations is wholly beyond reason in the present age.** The answer to the world's difficulties is not the old destructive reactionary policy of arming to the teeth, but of so building our national edifices and so relating them one to the other that we can at once by mutual organization of nations reduce the premiums to a minimum, or wipe them out altogether by building a concrete fireproof structure of internationalism—equipped with such lightning rods as world courts and international parliaments, and, if needs must be, an international police force of volunteers.

What to-day—what single thing—would most quickly win for Germany anew the good will of the world and make possible the immediate coming of peace abroad? What else but an announcement by Germany that hereafter she would forever abandon universal military service? The chief menace of her militarism, against which all the world is roused, would disappear over-night.

No, to lead the world aright, the United States ought not to be debating to-day whether it prefers voluntary military training or universal conscription, but how rapidly it can induce the other nations by precept, by example, by enlightened leadership, to limit all armaments to the dimensions of police forces. Fortunately, there is evidence in every land that the world is to be a different place when the soldiers return from the trenches.

"Upon the outcome of the great debate on 'Conscription *vs.* Democracy' depends the
estion whether the last fortress of democracy in the world and the greatest adventure
human history shall go down in failure."—*George W. Nasmyth.*

Universal Military Training and Democracy

By

GEORGE NASMYTH, Ph.D.

Author of

"Social Progress and the Darwinian Theory: A Study of Force as a Factor in Human Relations"

Although a great deal has been said to suggest that this country was considering merely the adoption of a harmless system of compulsory military training resembling the so-called Swiss system, the fact remains that at no time has any bill been introduced in Congress based upon the Swiss or militia system; the two Chamberlain bills, the so-called Moseley bill and the General Staff bill have all been based upon the Prussian system in which the youth is placed under centralized military control, deprived of his civilian rights and placed at enforced military labor for a prolonged period. The General Staff now asks for nine months' military training but adds that ultimately we must have two years if our soldiers and armies are to be "adequately trained." See *A Proper Military Policy for the United States* by the General Staff, War Department, Washington, D. C.

AMERICAN UNION AGAINST MILITARISM

Weatory Building   **Washington, D. C.**

"MILITARISM: the spirit and temper which exalts the military virtues and ideals
minimizes the defects of military training and the cost of war and preparation for it."—
bster's International Dictionary, 1915.

AMERICAN
UNION AGAINST
MILITARISM

---

*Opposed to the Adoption of a Permanent System of
Universal Military Training and Service*

OFFICERS

OSWALD GARRISON VILLARD, *Chairman*
AMOS R. E. PINCHOT, *Vice Chairman*
AGNES BROWN LEACH, *Treasurer*
CHARLES T. HALLINAN, *Executive Secretary*

EXECUTIVE COMMITTEE

EMILY G. BALCH
A. A. BERLE
HERBERT S. BIGELOW
CRYSTAL EASTMAN
JOHN LOVEJOY ELLIOTT
EDMUND C. EVANS
ZONA GALE

OWEN R. LOVEJOY
JAMES H. MAURER
MARY McMURTRIE
HENRY R. MUSSEY
MARY WHITE OVINGTON
JOHN HAYNES HOLMES
ALEXANDER TRACHTENBERG

Send us your name, and a contribution if you can.

HEADQUARTERS
203 Westory Building, Washington, D. C.
Telephone Franklin 5930.

The Nation Press, Inc., New York

UNIVERSAL MILITARY TRAINING AND DEMOCRACY

By George Nasmyth, Ph.D., author of "Social Progress and the Darwinian Theory: A Study of Force as a Factor in Human Relations"

If any person had predicted two years ago that the people of America would be seriously discussing today the adoption of universal military training, he would have been looked upon as a visionary. But since the outbreak of the war in Europe, the rising tide of reaction which resulted from the international reign of terror; the increasing power of militarism in the world; and the great preparedness campaign which was carried to a successful conclusion in 1915 and 1916, have led, step by step, to an increasing agitation for universal military training, as an essential part of the system of national defense.

The advocates of universal military service are not limited to military officers, like General Leonard A. Wood,[1] or to partisans of a "big stick" policy in dealing with other nations, like Colonel Roosevelt. The growing importance of the subject is witnessed by the recent accession to their ranks of various college presidents, and of Prof. Ralph Barton Perry,[2] who has attempted to show that democracy has nothing to fear from universal military service.

Moreover, laws have actually been passed in the closing hours of the session of the legislature in New York State providing for military training in the high school, and universal military

---

[1] *The Military Obligations of Citizenship.* Princeton University Press 1915.

[2] *The Free Man and the Soldier*, by Prof. Ralph Barton Perry. *Scribner's*, 1916.

service for all young men between the ages of 18 and 21.[3] Finally the national defense act passed by the United States Congress in July, 1916,[4] gives to the military authorities the power to "draft" men into the army whenever voluntary enlistments shall be insufficient, so that universal military service or conscription, to use a more convenient term for the same idea, has been established as a legal principle in the Empire State and in the nation.

The fact that these laws were passed in the closing hours of legislative sessions, without adequate discussion and without complete understanding on the part of the people of the issues involved, makes it inevitable that the debate shall be re-opened in the near future. The principle at issue is fundamental in a democracy, and the most wide-spread discussion of the subject should be welcomed by all who believe in the power of an enlightened public opinion to decide rightly on fundamental principles.

UNIVERSAL MILITARY TRAINING AND PREPAREDNESS

The case for universal military training rests on entirely different grounds than does the general case for preparedness. If we did not have our other five lines of national defense which protect us from any attack from European or Asiatic powers, there might be some justification in this universal military service in America. But with two oceans, one 3000 and the other 5000 miles in width; the navy, the second largest in the world; submarines, which makes the transport of large bodies of troops across great distances a most hazardous undertaking; automatic and electric contact mines and coast fortifications, like those which made it impossible for the Allies successfully to land troops on the shores of Germany or even Turkey, even when the Allies were backed by a naval force three or four times greater than that of the Central European Powers—with all

---

[3] For the provisions of the Slater Bill and other bills for compulsory military training in New York send to the New York State Military Training Commission, Albany, N. Y.

[4] For the details of the method by which the "draft joker" was inserted in the permanent National Defense Act, see Rep. George Huddleston's speech in the *Congressional Record* for Sept. 5, 1916.

these first lines of defense, not even the most fearful and extreme of our militarists pretend that an army of seven to ten million men, which the system of universal military service would give us after a few years of building up reserves who had passed through the military machine, would be necessary to repel an actual invasion on American soil. Even Colonel Roosevelt did not demand a standing army of more than 250,000 men and a reserve army of 400,000 men to meet his requirements for an "adequate" national defense, and no one has seriously urged that our preparedness needs require an army of universal service proportions.

But the volunteer system will fail, it is urged. Even the standing army of 250,000 men and the militia of 400,000, provided for in the national defense act, cannot be raised by the voluntary method.

An Army of Social Service

If this force is needed, it can be raised by the right kind of an appeal to the American people. This involves a fundamental transformation of an army from its old-world character of a machine trained solely for wholesale murder, to a new world of social service. An army of labor trained in the work of reforestation, of irrigation, of building great highways, instructed in methods of camp sanitation and effective cooperation; from which every man would come out a more useful member of society and a more productive economic unit, would make a far different appeal to American young men than the standing army on the present system, or even a national guard of the socially elite. With this employment in useful production should go adequate compensation, just as there goes adequate compensation for police work, for the work of firemen and life-savers. Under a really democratic system of social service, such as this, there will be no difficulty in finding all the men that are needed, without resort to conscription.

But since the case which can be made out for compulsory service is so weak from the point of view of military necessity, its advocates fall back on other arguments. Universal military service, they claim, will promote democracy; it will unify the nation; it will increase patriotism; it will form greatly needed habits of obedience and discipline. These arguments constitute, in brief, the case for conscription, around which the great debate will rage, and they are so important that they should be subjected to the most searching analysis.

DEMOCRACY

Does universal military service involve equal sacrifice on the part of rich and poor alike? If both are killed, of course, both have made the last great sacrifice, and so far as their individual lives are concerned, it is equal. But for the families of the two men the difference is very great. For the family of the poor man, the loss of the bread-winner means that the widow must go out to work, that the children must be deprived of an opportunity for education, that their whole lives must be limited because they did not have the opportunity they would have had if their father had lived. For the rich man, on the contrary, no such sacrifice on the part of his family is involved. His wife is not compelled to go out and work, his children are not deprived of the opportunity of receiving a liberal education. If a conscription of wealth were advocated as a companion measure to a conscription of lives, there might be some justification for the argument on a basis of democracy. But a conscription of lives alone, such as is advocated by the believers in universal military service, is fundamentally unjust, if the family, instead of the individual, is considered as the real unit and the foundation of the nation's life.

Even if sacrifice of life is not involved, the sacrifice of time required for universal military service imposes an unequal burden upon the rich and the poor. For the rich man, Plattsburg is an enjoyable vacation, and a longer period of military service would not be any great hardship, but for the poor man it means a definite interruption of his economic life, the stopping of his earnings, a postponement of the time when he can afford to marry, an interruption of his difficult task of getting a foothold in his trade or small business. In Germany, it is estimated that the economic loss involved in taking a young man from the farm, for example, is equivalent to about $500 a year, and the father has to hire Polish or Italian laborers to take the place of the son who goes to serve for two years in the Kaiser's army, but for the rich man, military service offers a career, an entrance to the ranks of society, the opening of positions in the government service and educational advantages of technical training in the officers' colleges. No element of equality of sacrifice can be discovered in the two cases.

Those who believe that class distinctions can be broken down and democracy created by regimenting men into masses and forcing them to drill together, have missed the central idea of democracy, which is based on the principle of voluntary co-operation, of equality of opportunity, and the abolition of caste privileges. Those who believe that democracy can be imposed from without by force, and point to the example of France and Switzerland, should analyze the conditions in those countries more deeply. As soon as we penetrate below the surface, we find in each of them a great conflict between the forces of militarism and democracy. This conflict rages in all countries where universal military service is established, and it has been revealed in all its bitterness by the vivid, lightning flashes of the Dreyfus affair in France, the Zabern incident in Germany, and the Ulster crisis in the British army—all parallel instances of successful struggles for the supremacy of the military over the civil powers of government. In France the *revanche* movement which brought about the Russo-French Alliance, the three year conscription law of 1912, and the outcome of the Morocco crisis of 1911, all represented victories of the military caste over the forces of democracy and the popular government.

Switzerland has not had an aggressive militarism of the Pan-German type, it is true, but this is not due to any lack of desire on the part of the Swiss military officers who are like military officers the world over. It has been due to the fact that

Switzerland is a small country and any propaganda for a career of "national destiny," or the conquest of the world would render its advocates ludicrous. The military spirit, however, and its fundamental opposition to democracy is essentially the same in Switzerland as in Germany or France, as is witnessed, for example, by the testimony of Swiss Social Democrats at the International Socialist Congresses[6] in Stuttgart and other centers.

Everywhere militarism has been the most formidable enemy of democracy. For every million soldiers you must have at least 30,000 officers, and these 30,000 officers must make the military profession their life work. They must cultivate an iron will and a spirit of domination as essential elements of success, and necessarily they chafe with impatience at the discussions and restraints of democracy and the civil powers of government. Altogether they constitute a source of ever present danger to the peace of a nation which is powerful enough to be a menace to the world.

The testimony of representative British and German statesmen—Viscount Bryce, former Ambassador to America, and of Bismarck himself, is illuminating in this connection.

The reason why we have had one hundred years of peace in the English speaking world, according to Viscount Bryce, is because we have had so little militarism in America in the past. In the introduction to Professor Dunning's book on *The British Empire and the United States*, Bryce says that during a number of years the American masses would not have opposed war with England but "fortunately . . . the country was free from a pernicious military caste which worked such frightful evil in Europe, being indeed driven to desire opportunities for practising the work for which the profession exists."

This is the testimony of a British statesman. On the other hand Bismarck in his *Reflections and Reminiscences*, Chapter

* See *The Socialism of Today*, 1916 (Henry Holt and Company), pp. 614. "The Swiss comrades pointed out that their militia was commanded by officers of the ruling class and was used by the bourgeoisie against the working people." Report of the International Socialist Congress at Stuttgart in 1907.

XXII, tells us definitely how the Prussian militarists tried to push him into war, how he used this militarist pressure to throw the country into war with Austria in 1866, and with France in 1870, and how he had to resist the powerful militarist pressure towards war in 1867, in 1875 and on other occasions. Bismarck says on page 102, Volume ii:

It is natural that in the staff of the army not only younger active officers, but likewise experienced strategists, should feel the need of turning to account the efficiency of the troops led by them, and their own capacity to lead, and of making them prominent in history. It would be a matter of regret if this effect of the military spirit did not exist in the army; the task of keeping its results within such limits as the nations' need of peace can justly claim, is the duty of the political, not the military, heads of the state.

That at the time of the Luxemburg question, during the crisis of 1875, invented by Gortchakoff and France, and even down to the most recent times, the staff and its leaders have allowed themselves to be led astray and to endanger peace, lies in the very spirit of the institution.

If the breakdown of civilization in Europe has anything to teach America, surely it is the danger of any increase in the forces or the philosophy of militarism.

DISCIPLINE

The second argument for universal military training is that it will promote discipline. It will teach obedience and respect for authority, it is urged, and these elements are greatly needed in American life. The trouble here is the kind of discipline which military training provides. It is a discipline enforced from without and breaks down as soon as the restraining force is removed.[7] The whole object of military training is to secure

---

[7] It is certainly significant that in spite of New York City's vast conglomerate population, in spite of the intense feeling, for and against, aroused by our entrance into the war and by the draft, the only two mobs with which the police force of New York City have had to contend since our entrance into the war have both been composed wholly of soldiers and sailors. See *"Soldiers Storm 10,000 Socialists at Madison Square"* in New York *Tribune*, Nov. 26, 1918. See, for account of second riot by soldiers and sailors, the New York *Times* of Nov. 27, 1918. That even the Army officers tend to abandon discipline "when the restraining force is removed" even to the extent of neglecting their sworn duties, is clear from the remarkable statement made by Major-General David C. Shanks, in charge of the Port of Embarkation at Hoboken, New Jersey. See *"Shanks Accuses Army Officers of Lax Discipline"* in New York *Times*, Jan. 6, 1919.—Note by A. U. A. M.

instantaneous obedience without thought, to make a man a part
of an automatic military machine so that if he is ordered to
sink the *Lusitania* or destroy the city of Louvain, he will obey
instantly and unquestionably. Such unthinking obedience is far
removed from the self-imposed discipline, that respect for laws
because they have been enacted by common consent and for the
welfare of the people; of freedom of discussion, of speech, of
press, of assembly, and of conscience, which are the foundation stones of a self-governing democracy.[8] The history of
Prussia illustrates clearly the inevitable results of military discipline. At first, the German people opposed conscription bit-
terly, but after a few generations of men had been put through
the military machine and taught the right kind of obedience,
all opposition ceased. Germany became a servile state. More
and more power was given into the hands of the military caste,
and the events which have occurred since August 1, 1914, have
well been called "The Nemesis of Docility."

NATIONAL UNITY

The third argument is that it will promote Americanism, it
will heal all our divisions of race and nationality, eliminate the
hyphen, and unify the American people.

The experience of European nations which have tried to
meet similar problems by this method is in flat contradiction to
such an assumption. In Austria militarism has reigned with
undisputed sway, but universal military service for generations
has failed to unite Germans and Bohemians, Poles and Czechs
and Slavs in the ideal unity which our militarists picture for us
as the inevitable result of conscription. The history of Poland,
of the subject races and nationalities of Russia, and of Turkey,

---

[8] See an excellent article on educational aspects of the subject by Prof.
John Dewey in *The New Republic*, April 15, 1916.

See also publications of the American Union Against Militarism, Westory
building, Washington, D. C.:

(a) *New Jersey says "No"*; *Report of New Jersey Commission on Military Training in High Schools.*

(b) *Military Training in the Making of Men*, by Frederick J. Libby.

(c) *Universal Military Training; Our Latest Cure-all*, by Oswald
Garrison Villard.

(d) *Since the Night We Entered War.*

is a refutation of the claim that national unity can be secured by universal military service.

America needs unity, a national consciousness, and a national will, but no reactionary, militaristic, obsolete, Old World instrument, such as conscription, can unify the American people.

PATRIOTISM

A fourth argument for universal military training is that it will promote patriotism, it will teach a man to be ready to sacrifice himself for others and to lay down his life for his country in the service of a great idea. The difficulty with this plan is that there are various kinds of patriotism, and the tendency of militarism is to emphasize the wrong kind—the patriotism which corresponds to a narrow nationalism and to Jingoism and the patriotism which is based upon the hatred of other parts of the human race who happen to live the other side of a boundary line. Patriotism and nationalism of the wrong kind are defeating their own ends in Europe. For the sake of our country, as well as for humanity, we must develop another type of patriotism than universal military service has given us in Germany or in any of the European countries, a patriotism which will look upon America as a part of the world and will take pride in the contributions which America can make to the family of nations. Independence for the sake of independence, a new nation merely that there might be one more army and navy in the world, was no part of the purpose of the founders of the Republic. As Henry Adams said of the great author of the Declaration of Independence:

Jefferson aspired beyond the ambition of a nationality, and embraced in his view the whole future of man. That the United States should become a nation like France, England or Russia, or should conquer the world like Rome, was no part of his scheme. He wished to begin a new era. Hoping for a time when the world's ruling interests should cease to be local and should become universal; when questions of boundary and nationality should become insignificant; when armies and navies should be reduced to the work of police,—he set himself to the task of governing with this golden age in view. . . . He would not consent to build up a new nationality merely to create more navies and armies, to perpetuate the crimes and follies of Europe; the central government at Washington should not be permitted to indulge in the miserable ambitions that had made the Old World a hell and frustrated the hopes of humanity.

We need greatly a rebirth of true patriotism, just as we need a more fundamental democracy, deeper national unity, more self-discipline, but universal military service is not the panacea for these ills. A true American patriotism can be created only by a return to the great principles of the founders of the Republic, a new vision of the mission of America in the world, a great world task such as the establishment of a League to Enforce Peace, calling for the sacrifice of old provincialisms and outworn traditions in the service of humanity, as a whole. In this way, under the great constructive leadership of a world statesman, America can be unified. In this way we may recover our vision of democracy and we may lead the world into a higher patriotism, purified in the fiery furnace of this world crisis. By these new paths which lead out into a future full of hope and service, it may be that in the coming years the soul of America will be born again into a new and larger life, but never by the path of conscription, of fear and servile obedience, and the mechanical methods of militarism.

A much deeper principle is involved than is usually discussed in connection with universal military service: What kind of a society do we wish to live in? For, if the principle of compulsion is accepted in the case of military service, it must logically be accepted for service in munition factories, on the railroads, in coal mines and in all industrial and economic life upon which modern wars depend. In other words, once having granted the principle of compulsion on the ground of military necessity, all the fundamental principles of democracy must be sacrificed and our country must be "Prussianized" from within. Freedom of speech, freedom of assembly and freedom of the press are all opposed to military effectiveness and must disappear step by step if freedom of conscience, the advance trench of democracy, is carried by the militarists; for in the last analysis, universal military service means conscription of conscience.[*]

The new political persecution represented by the adoption of conscription differs from the old religious persecution in this: Whereas, in the Middle Ages the heretic could save his life by keeping his mouth closed and his opinions to himself, in the modern political persecution of Twentieth Century militarism, the heretic who may believe that an aggressive foreign policy is unjust, or a war which his country has declared is unprovoked, is compelled not only to keep his opinions to himself, but is forced to go out and kill his fellowmen against whom he may have no cause for enmity whatever.

America is the only great nation left in the world in which militarism is not enthroned and the principle of conscription established. In order to defend our institutions and our democracy from imaginary dangers from without, we are urged to surrender to this much more real and formidable enemy of militarism and conscription from within. Upon the outcome of the great debate on "Conscription *vs.* Democracy" depends the question whether the last fortress of democracy in the world and the greatest adventure in human history shall go down in failure. All patriotic Americans, all who believe that America has a mission and a great message of democracy to give to the world should enroll themselves in defence of America's freedom and democratic institutions presenting a united front against this attempt to militarize the whole American people.

Sometime in the future, if Europe remains an armed camp after this war, and if militarism is enthroned in the world, it may become inevitable for America to adopt conscription, and, in Jefferson's words "to perpetuate the crimes and follies of Europe," "to indulge in the miserable ambitions that had made the Old World a hell and frustrated the hopes of humanity." But if conscription ever does become inevitable let us not add blasphemy to our other crimes by adopting militarism in the

---

[*] See Norman Angell's admirable article on the psychological aspect of universal military service as a conscription of conscience in *The New Republic*, April 8, 1916.

name of democracy. No, let us do it with the clear knowledge that we are dealing a death blow to the greatest experiment in democracy the human race has ever tried. Let us do it with the consciousness that we have participated in a great world tragedy, and that, with the triumph of militarism in the New World as well as the Old, we shall have seen government of the people, by the people and for the people, perish from the earth.

Compulsory Training
Views of a Military Expert

"If it were possible to exact military service in time of peace, it would not be wise. If it were exacted at all, it would have to be imposed upon all within a certain age limit, and the number of men to be trained would be immense. The men to train them would be few and only a minimum of time could be required. The results would be nil. Citizens would look upon it as an irksome duty and would discharge it in a perfunctory manner. Drawing men by lots, as we draw juries, would be absolutely inimical to our institutions.

"Compulsory military service is, therefore, unwise and absolutely incompatible with our institutions. We must depend upon voluntary enlistments for the making of our [peace time] armies. Our service must be sufficiently remunerative, beneficial and attractive to draw men."

[Lieut. James J. Mayes, U. S. Army, winner of the gold medal for the best essay on "What Legal Exaction of Military Service on the part of the Government is Wise and Compatible with Our Institutions," offered by the Military Service Institution of the United States. Published in the Journal of the Institution, March-April, 1910.]

Militarizing Our Youth

*The Significance of the Reserve Officers'
Training Corps in our
Schools and Colleges*

By

ROSWELL P. BARNES

WITH AN

INTRODUCTION

By

JOHN DEWEY

൭ശ

A sequel to the pamphlet by Winthrop D. Lane
on Military Training in Schools and Colleges
of the United States

൭ശ

COMMITTEE ON MILITARISM IN EDUCATION
387 Bible House, Astor Place, New York City
1 9 2 7

"SIZE DOESN'T NECESSARILY MAKE SOLDIERS."

The above picture (not including the two figures at the left) appeared with the given title in the *Kansas City* (*Mo.*) *Star* of October 10th, 1926. The boys are drilling in the R. O. T. C. unit of Paseo high school. The ages range from 18 to 18 years.

INTRODUCTION

Is the reader aware that there is in existence in this country a well-organized movement to militarize the tone and temper of our national life? Is he aware that militarism has already become a vested interest, economic as well as political and social? Is he aware that the effort of this vested interest to militarize the country is operating deliberately and knowingly through the medium of our schools and colleges? Is he aware that the vested interest resorts to methods of aspersion and overt attack in order to intimidate those persons and organizations who oppose its efforts to get a strangle hold on our schools and in order to prevent students from being influenced by the facts and arguments these opponents present? Is he aware that, by their own statements, their present intervention—not to call it by the name of interference—in education is regarded by the vested militaristic interest as simply the best substitute attainable at the present time for universal military service and as a step in creating conditions when conscriptive service will be adopted?

The following pages give material that enables anyone to make up his mind about these questions. The material is in the form not of the reckless aspersions in which the militaristic crowd freely indulges but in the form of facts, readily verifiable, most of them cited from official sources. It is doubtless this element of fact, undeniable fact, which so arouses the bitterness of the vested militaristic interest, and leads it in the words of one of its representatives, quoted in this pamphlet, to urge attack upon "subversive agitation" not only with "facts and figures" but with "venom and fury". The attack on the fifty-four persons who endorsed the previous (Lane) report of the society which sponsors also the present report was certainly long on venom and fury, but short on facts and figures—except figures of speech.

The American people is not as yet sufficiently militarized to favor a movement for its complete assimilation of the military spirit. The danger is that it will not be aware of what is going on. Hence the importance, the supreme importance, of stating the facts which will enable our people to become aware of the present organized movement, and, in being aware, to check it. Hence also the venom and fury directed against those who have become acquainted with the facts and who are striving to give the American public a knowledge of them. ' Nothing will be as fatal to the success of the militaristic attempt as knowledge of the facts. To suppress the dissemination of this knowledge is the logical course for the militaristic interest to pursue. Their previous activity shows that it considers one of the most effective means of suppression to be zeal in discrediting those who make the facts known by any kind of disingenuous and misleading statement. The publication of the present report will doubtless lead to the renewal of statements of which Roosevelt's "short and ugly word" is the fitting appelation.

For our part, we invite the attention of the public to the *facts,* secure in the confidence of what the outcome will be if the attention of the public is once given them. But unless the facts are known and attended to, the outcome is by no means so certain. The militaristic movement is well organized, is energetically active, unrelentingly aggressive. It has a definite program and is taking definite steps for its execution. The nature of the program and of the steps in its execution are set forth on the authority of official documents in the pages of this pamphlet. Peoples do not become militaristic or imperialistic because they deliberately choose so to do. They become militaristic gradually and unconsciously in response to conditions of which militarism is the final consequence. Education of youth and the reflex of that education on parents and friends is an important part of the forces which have militarization for their consequence.

Of this situation the militaristic vested interest is well apprized. Are those who are opposed to the subordination of our civil policies to a warlike purpose equally aware of it? What are they doing and going to do about it?

JOHN DEWEY.

PRUSSIAN OF 1912 OR AMERICAN OF 1927?

The following statements of basic philosophy are from the Prussian General Friedrich von Bernhardi's "Germany and the Next War" (1912), from U. S. War Department Training Regulations, and from R. O. T. C. textbooks in use today in our public schools and colleges. Try to distinguish the Prussian from the American and then look up the sources of the quotations in the Key at the bottom of the next page.

1. "We live in a world governed by Divine laws which we can neither alter nor evade. And in this world of ours force is the ultimate power."

2. "Between States the only check on injustice is force, and in morality and civilization each people must play its own part and promote its own ends and ideals."

3. "During the course of a great war every government, whatever its previous form, should become a despotism."

4. "The object to be attained by training is to enable the Army to wage offensive warfare. While training must cover certain phases of defensive doctrine and police doctrine, the Army must definitely understand that these are only means to the definite end—offensive warfare—and every individual in the military service must be imbued with the spirit of the offensive."

5. "An armistice should never be granted at the instance of a defeated foe. It is a confession of weakness, of inability to clinch the victory."

6. "Struggle is, therefore, a universal law of Nature, and the instinct of self-preservation which leads to struggle is acknowledged to be a natural condition of existence. 'Man is a fighter.' Self-sacrifice is a renunciation of life, whether in the existence of the individual or in the life of States, which are agglomerations of individuals. The first and paramount law is the assertion of one's own independent existence. By self-assertion alone can the State maintain the conditions of life for its citizens, and insure them the legal protection which each man is entitled to claim from it. This duty of self-assertion is by no means satisfied by the mere repulse of hostile attacks; it includes the obligation to assure the possibility of life and development to the whole body of the nation embraced by the State."

7. "The mainsprings of human action are self-preservation and self-interest, in a word *selfishness*—the 'touch of nature which makes the whole world kin'."

5

"EVERY BOY AN ENVOY FOR MILITARY PREPAREDNESS"

Texas has an annual R. O. T. C. day at the state fair, with student military units from all over the state, and some from Oklahoma, competing in drill. When the 1926 maneuvers were held on October 22nd, it was a holiday for all Dallas high schools, Much time had been spent in preparation,—some regular curriculum examinations, scheduled to be given a couple of days before Fair Day, were postponed because the boys had not had time to study. Companies were entered from Dallas, San Antonio, and Fort Worth high schools, from Oklahoma Military Academy and others,—thirteen companies in all, most of them high school units, at least one thirteen-year-old boy participating. There were drills, executed with mechanical precision; enthusiastic applause from girls, parents, and "pep squads" in the stands; an imposing silver loving cup on a table in the arena; army officers and competition judges reviewing in scrutinizing dignity.

The Dallas Morning News on the following day spread out five pictures along with columns of news stories, reporting "stands thronged", "military spectacle _ _ _ which overshadowed anything of its kind in the history of cadet competition", "giant silver cup _ _ _ presented _ _ _ with impressive ceremony", "awards of infantry sabres, and a handsome gold watch, _ _ _ cash awards of $75, _ _ _ cash prizes of $40, _ _ _ scholarships to Camp Dallas."

"PRUSSIAN OF 1912 OR AMERICAN OF 1927?"—Key to page 5.

1. *The R. O. T. C. Manual, Infantry, 2nd year advanced,* Vol. IV, 7th edition, August, 1925, page 207; and *Our Military Policy,* by P. S. Bond, Lieut. Colonel, U. S. Army, page 6.

2. *Germany and the Next War,* by General Friedrich von Bernhardi, 1912, page 20.

3. *The R. O. T. C. Manual, Infantry, 2nd year advanced,* Vol. IV, 7th edition, August, 1925, page 384; and *Our Military Policy* by P. S. Bond, Lieut. Colonel, U. S. Army, page 47.

4. *Training Regulations,* No. 10-5, War Department, December 23, 1921, *Doctrines, Principles, and Methods,* page 3.

5. *The R. O. T. C. Manual, Infantry, 2nd year advanced,* Vol. IV, 7th edition, August, 1925, page 255.

6. *Germany and the Next War,* by General Friedrich von Bernhardi, 1912, page 21.

7. *The R. O. T. C. Manual, Infantry, 2nd year advanced,* Vol. IV, 7th edition, August, 1925, page 208; and *Our Military Policy,* by P. S. Bond, Lieut. Colonel, Corps of Engineers, U. S. Army, page 7.

With such a situation before us we can understand the value of the R. O. T. C. from a military point of view as it is explained by Major Bloxham Wood, U. S. Army, who is quoted in a Dallas paper as saying, "The R. O. T. C. units in the high schools are the greatest factor making for military preparedness in this country, for they make every boy who takes such instruction an envoy for military preparedness. These boys in turn bring home the value and necessity of such training, even into homes that might otherwise be antagonistic."

A Dallas paper also quotes General Hinds, commander of the Eighth Corps Area, as taking the position that the most important work of the army at the present time is the building up of the R. O. T. C. in the schools.

The promotion, direct supervision, and ultimate control of this military training in public high schools by the military arm of the federal government is a new departure in American history. It is permitted under the National Defense Act of 1916, amended in 1920. Compulsory drill in colleges under the direct and final control of the War Department has also been promoted under this Act with unprecedented vigor.

THE PUBLIC IS ALARMED.

Certain dangers inherent in this military system were called to the attention of the American people less than two years ago in a pamphlet on Military Training in the Schools and Colleges of the United States, written by Winthrop D. Lane. There had been some previous sporadic interest in the matter; but during the last two years at least 66 organizations (23 of national scope— see list on page 39) representing large and influential sections of our citizenship have given serious study to the situation and have expressed alarm. The most important organizations in the church, in labor, in education and social service have expressed disapproval and have met with bitter condemnation by military and military-minded groups.

Interest in militarism in education has become world-wide. In England, for example, a member of Parliament has published a pamphlet on the problem, in which he writes:

"In the United States of America a great effort is being made to get the War Office out of the schools. We join wholeheartedly in a like campaign. It is in the schools, in the shaping of young minds, that the foundations of wars are laid."[1*]

*References are listed together on Page 47.

WHAT DOES "MILITARISM" MEAN?

Many citizens deprecate this whole development as "militaristic". They deplore the departure from the historic policies of America. The military group, on the other hand, scorns those policies as ineffective and dangerous. There has been heated debate, as well as reasonable discussion, as to what constitutes militarism. We use, therefore, a non-partisan definition. Webster's dictionary is the authority:

Militarism

1. A military state or condition; disposition to provide for the strength and safety of a nation or government by maintaining strong military forces.

2. The spirit and temper which exalts the military virtues and ideals and minimizes the defects of military training and the cost of war and preparation for it:—often used derogatorily of the spirit which tends to confer undue privilege or prominence on the military class.

WARNING FROM LEGISLATORS.

The protest against the Reserve Officers' Training Corps is based upon the fear that a caste is being developed which, in the dictionary meaning of the word, is *militaristic*. There seems to be a reasonable basis for such fear, because congressional committees on military and naval affairs both point out such a danger. The Committee on Appropriations for the Navy Department (for 1927) included in its Report to the House of Representatives the following section:

"RESERVES GENERALLY"

"The committee believes that the attention of the House should be called to the reserve situation generally. That the reserves have a necessary and important place in our scheme of national defense there is no question. That there should be a limit, however, there should be no question. To keep it within the proper limits under existing law seems to fall to the lot of this committee, which should not be. *Unless it is watched and closely watched it will expand to the point where we will have accomplished by indirection what we have always striven to avoid directly, and that is the establishment of a large force in this country possessing military views and tendencies which will outnumber and outweigh in voice our regular establishments. This is not believed to be an over-statement of what may be reasonably expected if we should fail to watch the situation closely . . .* "[2] (Italics supplied.)

When Brigadier General Delafield, President of the Reserve Officers' Association of the United States, appeared before the House committee on military appropriations to ask for larger

8

sums for Reserve expenditures for 1927 the Chairman, Mr. Anthony, made this statement, which is captioned *"Propaganda for Increased Appropriations"*:

"So far as I am concerned, I want to be very frank with you in my attitude toward these appropriations. It is the purpose of this committee to be as fair as we can in the consideration of these Organized Reserve items, but as one member of the committee I very strenuously object to the system which is apparently in vogue of, year after year, bringing outside pressure to bear on this committee for the purpose of increasing the appropriations for these items. We are glad to have you appear in your official capacity to give us any information or to make any statement that you care to make to us but as a member of the committee *I do object to the systematic pressure that is brought upon this committee and upon Members of Congress year after year for this purpose. I think it sets a very bad precedent, and one that is liable to grow into a very vicious system if it is permitted to continue."*[3] (Italics supplied.)

The Reserve Officers' Training Corps must be examined in the light of these warnings from Congressional committees.

MILITARY PROGRAM NEW IN EXTENT AND NATURE.

In a fifteen year period (up to the last available statistics) federal expenditures on military training in civil schools have increased from \$725,168[4] to \$10,696,504,[5] a fifteen-fold increase; the number of institutions giving such training, from 57[6] to 223,[7] a four-fold increase; the army personnel detailed to conduct the training, from 85[8] to 1809,[9] an eighteen-fold increase; the number of students enrolled, from 29,979[10] to 119,914,[11] a four-fold increase. In 1916 there was one army officer to supervise the training at Ohio State University; the 1927 catalogue lists forty-four officers and enlisted men in the same university. (Compare these increases with the increase in population which has been but a 27% increase from 1910 to 1926.[12])

The intent and purpose of the program are avowedly new under the National Defense Act, and consequently its whole nature. The Adjutant General in his Report for 1920 pointed out the R. O. T. C. program as new:

"The Military Academy, [West Point] *for the first time in its existence* was placed in a position closely approximating competition with thousands of educational institutions all over the country which offer military training of a high order, though necessarily limited in scope, through units of the Reserve Officers' Training Corps." (Italics supplied.)[13]

Professor William Bradley Otis of the College of the City of New York, who was sent to France by the government in 1919 to explain to the A. E. F. the terms of the treaty of peace, and who was largely responsible for the passage of many state laws requiring a study of the U. S. Constitution as a requisite to a college degree, testified before the House Military Affairs Committee in 1926 in part as follows:

> "Never before, gentlemen, in American history has the freedom of our higher educational institutions been thus threatened by an Army bureaucracy. It is an insidious influence and has gained headway largely because the American people have not been aware of what is going on . . . I would like to have you notice this particularly: The freedom of faculties to determine their own curriculum has been invaded for the first time in the history of the country."[14]

Professor Otis characterized compulsory military training as "a peace-time conscription, utterly foreign to American ideals, utterly counter to American traditions."

The War Department statistics, the Adjutant General's report, and Professor Otis's statement, therefore, all go to show that we are dealing with a new issue.

TWO NEW EXTENSIONS WITHIN A YEAR.

1. In 1926 at the beginning of the academic year, the Navy Department established Naval R. O. T. C. units in six of the leading universities as an experiment. At the end of two months they announced that the "experiment" was successful and that the system would be expanded.[15]

II. The War Department within the last year has made plans for a new Munitions Battalion to be composed of college men recruited during their Junior year to spend a full year in the regular army studying the procurement needs of the Army and the methods of supplying those needs.[16]

THE TRAINING IS STRICTLY MILITARY.

The War Department's Regulations state:

> "The primary object of the Reserve Officers' Training Corps is to provide systematic military training at civil educational institutions for the purpose of qualifying selected students of such institutions for appointment as reserve officers in the military forces of the United States . . . "[17]

A college may have one unit, or it may have units in several branches of the service: artillery, infantry, cavalry, coast artillery, medical, engineering, air, etc.

The purpose of the R. O. T. C. under the National Defense Act, as amended, was explained by Secretary of War Weeks in 1921 as follows:

"Thus we find that the Reserve Officers' Training Corps has a more definite mission than was anticipated at the time of its inception. It was proposed then to prepare young men for an undefined service in the event of an emergency. It is proposed now, under the new law, to prepare young men to be officers in a definitely organized Citizen Army."[18]

But it is not presented to the parents as military training. As Winthrop D. Lane pointed out by quotations from manuals, the boys, and the officers who drill them, are told that "success in battle" is the end of military training; while the parents are told that the training "is not to make soldiers out of your boys."

AS THE CATALOGUES DESCRIBE THE TRAINING.

Cornell University.

"The aim of the Department of Military Science and Tactics is to give training which will enable graduates to serve effectively as officers of any forces raised by the United States.—The course includes physical training, military drill, and the application of fundamental principles of modern tactics.—The University provides pay, ranging from $75 to $250 annually for each of the commissioned officers of the Reserve Officers' Training Corps. In addition, the twenty-six senior officers are assistants in the department."

Davidson College.

"1st Year Basic Course

This course is designed to give the student a solid grounding in close order drill, military courtesy, military hygiene and first aid, physical drill and rifle marksmanship. One recitation and three hours field work, throughout the year. Credit three hours. Required for Freshmen.

2nd Year Basic Course

This course includes: Command and leadership, scouting and patrolling, musketry, interior guard duty, the mechanism and function of the Browning Automatic Rifle. One hour theoretical and three hours practical instruction per week. Credit three hours. Required for Sophomores."

University of Wyoming.

"Description of Courses—Basic—First year, 1a, 1b, 1c, Military fundamentals, practical and theoretical. Training in the duties of a private. Marksmanship, 15 hours; Military Courtesy, 3 hours; Military Hygiene and First Aid, 8 hours; Physical drill, 6 hours; Infantry Drill, Command and Leadership 64 hours. Total 96 hours."

"Second year...Scouting and Patrolling, 12 hours; Musketry, 10 hours; Interior Guard Duty, 4 hours; Automatic Rifle, 12 hours; Infantry Drill, Command, and Leadership, 58 hours. Total 96 hours."

OFFICIAL R. O. T. C. TEACHINGS.

From "R. O. T. C. Manual for Infantry, Second Year Advanced Volume IV", Seventh Edition by P. S. Bond.*

Page 387. "The prejudice against any form of compulsion in time of peace remained so strong that Congress promptly and unhesitatingly rejected all measures for universal training, thus declining to accept the most important lesson of the war." (World War.)

Pages, 395, 396. "The Defects of our Policy: (a) Reliance upon voluntary service which cannot produce the troops required for a major war.

(b) Direction of military operation by a civilian Secretary of War.

(c) Failure to recognize the obligation of the citizen to the state, and to adopt compulsory service in time of war and compulsory training in time of peace."

Page 390. "What Constitutes a Proper Military Policy for the U. S.:

(1) A Regular Army of about 300,000 enlisted men and 20,000 officers.

(2) A national guard under complete Federal control, numbering from 400,000 to 500,000 officers and men.

(3) An organized reserve of 500,000 to 1,000,000 officers and men.

(4) An unorganized reserve to consist of:
> (a) An officers' reserve corps, to include an unlimited number of individuals qualified as officers, to be drawn from the Reserve Officers' Training Corps and other available sources.

> (b) An enlisted reserve. . ." etc.

(5) The Reserve Officers' Training Corps in schools and colleges.

(6) Universal military training for young men in time of peace." etc.

In 1925, while the advocates of military training were protesting vehemently that its purpose was the inculcation of patriotism and the teaching of citizenship the students were learning in their manual, which is called on its fly leaf the "Military Bible":

"To finish an opponent who hangs on, or attempts to pull you to the ground, always try to break his hold by driving the knee or foot to his crotch and gouging his eyes with your thumbs."[19]

"This inherent desire to fight and kill must be carefully watched for and encouraged by the instructor."[20]

Some students at the College of the City of New York printed the above and other excerpts from the chapter on "The Spirit of the Bayonet" in Moss and Lang's Manual. Within a few weeks of the publication of these quotations, a general order was issued

---

*Note: Though some of this matter has been deleted from a recent edition of this particular manual, it is included in other texts by the same author and used by the R. O. T. C. at the present time.

from the War Department authorizing the discontinuance of bayonet combat in the R. O. T. C. The text books were called in, and "The Spirit of the Bayonet" expurgated. But why? Of what use to emasculate Mars on the drill field when it cannot be done on the battlefield? Will the War Department coach its pupils for a romantic game of glittering parades?

Is not the army officer more logical whose article, "Uplift Hits the Army", was carried by the Army and Navy Register for July 25, 1925? He protests:

> "Good citizenship is an excellent thing, and so are religion, filial affection, and brotherly love. But they are not the ends of an army. An army exists to kill men, when ordered, in the nation's quarrel irrespective of its justice. . . If we want an army, we should recognize it for what it is. We should not tell lies about its being a school for citizenship or manual training, nor clutter up its drill grounds with disciples of these irrelevant arts."

WHAT MAKES MILITARISM?

For a basic definition of militarism, we have already used Webster's Dictionary as our authority. But we must analyze the war system in connection with our definition. According to Professor George A. Coe:

> "War is, of course, a state of mind. This means not merely the mental processes that accompany and immediately precede hostilities, but also the entire set of readinesses that determine, in advance of acute friction, how a nation shall conduct itself with relation to friction-producing causes. Habits of thought and sentiment, which I shall here call the national mind-set, may and do make war while there is yet peace. They make it, not by hating other nations, not by desiring war, but by adjusting the whole mental mechanism so that, in certain situations, war-favoring reactions will occur as a matter of course. War seems to break upon us like an electric storm or an earthquake; it seems to happen *to* us. But, in reality it happens *in* us, as a long, inter-connected series of events, the last of which—the call to arms and actual fighting—merely carries out the nature of the series."[21]

A. MILITARY FATALISM.

One of the postulates to the development of a mind-set that will facilitate war responses is the belief that war is "inevitable". Perhaps the greatest obstacle to social progress is the acceptance of any evil of society as inevitable; the attitude that inasmuch as it has been in the past, and is now, it ever shall be, world without end. This was the argument used against those who fought dueling and slavery. Those evils were said to be the result of tendencies which are a part of "human nature as God ordained it." Thus, in 1858, arguing for slavery, Reverend W. G. Brownlow said in a public debate:

13

"Not only will I throughout this discussion openly and boldly take the ground that slavery as it exists in America ought to be perpetuated, but that slavery is an established and inevitable condition of human society. I will maintain the ground that God always intended the relation of master and slave to exist, that slavery having existed ever since the first organization of society, it will exist to the end of time."

The training textbooks and the lectures on military policy give such an interpretation to history as will tend to establish in the students' minds the inevitability and the efficacy of the war system.

Major McNair, the commandant of the Purdue University R. O. T. C., wrote in the Purdue Alumnus, May 3rd, 1926:

"If a Pacifist is one who believes that war is unnecessary and preventable, then pacifism becomes a menace."

B. MILITARY COERCION.

Even more suggestive of Old World autocracy than militaristic teachings, is the use of compulsion by the military. The arm of the war machine which reaches into the university with coercive authority is, in many institutions, practically inescapable as far as the student is concerned. He consequently goes out into the world having had as his only experience with the war system an experience in which there was no choice but to submit to it. Anyone who questions it is jeered as unpatriotic, queer, or lily-livered, and peremptorily crushed to subjection or else banished as undeserving of the benefits of education. The war system has thus been inevitable and real in the student's personal experience. Appeal to reason or compromise has been ruled out. Force has been the ultimate power. And this experience is likely to be a more important factor than classroom theory in determining the attitude of the student now and in the future toward such questions as disarmament, and the practicability of arbitration or treaties for the outlawry of war.

C. MILITARY "STATESMANSHIP."

This education tends to destroy interest and faith in substitutes for war in settling disputes. Moreover, sound military strategy teaches that the best defense is a quick offense. When relations with other nations become strained, there is always a difference of opinion as to what policy is best for the United States. In such controversies, those who have been submitted to the experience of compulsory military training are prejudiced. The fact that they may have been taught that war is hell is not a real deterrent; because they have been led at the same time to believe

14

that it is inevitable. Therefore, in their reasoning, the sooner force is used, the less hell will there be.

How many R. O. T. C. commandants or other professional military men urged arbitration of our disputes with Mexico over oil lands? We have not heard of many! But numbers of history and law professors did, and enough of the public to influence the State Department. Arbitration is obviously not the military way of doing things.

"No one is more opposed to war than is a military man"; but when it comes to developing a substitute for it,—arbitration, the League of Nations, the World Court, the outlawry of war,—he is apt to consider them all "devitalizing" suggestions to be summarily disposed of. The Army and Navy Journal (officially recommended by the War Department for use in the R. O. T. C.) on July 2, 1927, explained the military attitude toward M. Briand's proposal from France:

> "The proposal to outlaw war is one of those projects which appeal specially to a nation seeking an object not revealed on first presentation. To the pacifist and the unthinking, it 'has a pleasant tinkling sound foreannouncing the fruition of that wonderful idea of the Brotherhood of Man of which Tennyson sang so sweetly half a century ago. But to the hard-headed practical statesman who is unwilling to jeopardize the vital interest of America, who is confronted by the specific declaration of the Constitution reserving the war-making power to Congress, and who is indisposed to permit the United States to be drawn into foreign entanglements, it has a harsh raucous note which cries 'Danger!' We doubt if the Administration will negotiate any such pacts, and if it does—well, the Senate will dispose of them as it did of the League of Nations."

D. MILITARY SUPPRESSION.

Abridgment of free speech on political issues and interference with academic freedom were essential features of the regimes of Napoleon, of Metternich, of Bismarck, and other autocracies. But Americans, especially in the early days, have persistently been on guard against the use of these methods by any agency whatsoever. And such methods of suppression are especially insidious and difficult to combat when they are linked up with the military arm of the federal government reaching into civil educational institutions with the prestige of national and coercive authority. That this is a new feature of American democracy has already been demonstrated.

This matter is so close to the heart of the R. O. T. C. system that we must cite specific instances. Winthrop D. Lane, in his pamphlet referred to above, pointed out several cases of interference with academic freedom. The following is an exhibit of 10 other typical cases in which we mention names and places:

TEN EXAMPLES OF MILITARY-ACADEMIC SUPPRESSION.

1. *Ohio State University:* Donald Timerman, student pastor of the Methodist Church, and Reserve Chaplain, was recommended for discharge by the R. O. T. C. commandant, Colonel A. M. Shipp, for stating in public that he did not believe in compulsory military training. Scabbard and Blade criticized his remarks as "traitorous to the society, disrespectful to the country and unfitting as a member of the Officers' Reserve Corps." (Columbus Dispatch, February 16, 1927.) Investigation was opened before a board appointed by the Corps Area Commandant. Protest against this interference with Rev. Timerman's freedom of utterance was made at Washington and the War Department finally ordered that no further action be taken.

2. *University of Hawaii:* President D. L. Crawford issued a signed statement February 9th, 1927, upholding compulsory drill, and concluded: "Further discussion of this subject therefore will be fruitless and will avail nothing. If certain students find the situation too irksome they have the privilege of withdrawing from the university."

3. *West Chester, (Pa.) Normal College:* The Bernhard F. Schlegel Post of the American Legion and the County Committee of the Legion claim credit for bringing about the dismissal of two members of the faculty, Prof. Robert Kerlin and Prof. John Kinneman, who supported the right of the student liberal club to discuss and criticize the policy of our government in Nicaragua and Mexico.

4. *University of Nebraska:* A State Citizens' Committee of One Hundred was organized in 1926 to advocate the abolition of compulsory R. O. T. C. at the university. Rev. Harry Huntington, Methodist student pastor at the university, was chairman, and two other student pastors and the Y. M. C. A. secretary, Mr. Arthur Jorgensen, were active in it. When the issue was being discussed in the university community, the Board of Regents issued this statement:

March 20, 1926.

"The Board disapproves the attitude of certain religious and welfare workers assigned to the university who do not seem to realize the gross impropriety of accepting the good will and hospitality of the institution and conducting from offices, given them by the Regents, a campaign against the traditional policies of the institution and against the authority of the governing body. The Regents respectfully suggest

16

that all churches and societies assigning religious and welfare workers to the institution select only those who will cooperate with the university authorities in maintaining the policies of the school."

Mr. Jorgensen has since seen fit to "resign".

5. *University of Georgia*: Paul Guthrie is no longer Y. M. C. A. secretary at the University of Georgia. He was too "radical" because he was opposed to compulsory drill and organized an Interracial Committee which promoted goodwill between whites and colored. The student paper, although it opposed some of his policies denounced "the movement to fire Paul Guthrie from the University on account of his holding a few trifling opinions."

6. *Oklahoma University*: George Chase Lewis, Lieut. Colonel U. S. Infantry, Oklahoma City, wrote to President Bizzell at the university in connection with a proposed engagement for Rev. John Nevin Sayre to speak at the university at a meeting arranged by opponents of compulsory drill. After characterizing Mr. Sayre as one who "pretends to be strictly religious", but who is more dangerous than an open communist, his letter concludes: "I trust you will be able to curtail pernicious activities at Norman", (the University town). Mr. Sayre was not given opportunity to speak on the university grounds, but a local church consented to the use of its building for Mr. Sayre's meeting.

7. *Washington, D. C., High School*: Major General Amos A. Fries, Chief of the Chemical Warfare Service of the Army, demanded the removal from the high school faculty of Dr. Henry Flury who wrote a definition of socialism which won a five dollar prize in a contest conducted by the Forum magazine. General Fries objected to the ideas set forth in the definition. The Board of Education did not dismiss Dr. Flury.

8. *Agnes Scott College, Decatur, Ga.*: An invitation to Mrs. Lucia Ames Mead to speak in the chapel of Agnes Scott College was cancelled on December 4th, 1926, following protests of Mr. Asa Warren Candler, President of the Argonne Post of the American Legion against the presentation of the ideas of the "youth movement for peace", and calling Mrs. Mead a "Red and a Bolshevik". (The Congregationalist, Dec. 30, 1926.)

9. *Boston University in 1925*: Dean Everett W. Lord forced the resignation of Miss Henrietta Perkins, editor of the Boston University "Bean Pot" for satirizing compulsory R. O. T. C. (Compulsory feature abolished in 1926 by President Marsh.)

Dean Lord wrote: "You have adopted the tone of the pacifist, the slacker, the renegade, and the traitor . . . I shall, therefore, refuse to permit another issue of the Beanpot unless the entire editorial board is changed . . . I shall ask Dean Warren to discuss your standing with the faculty of the College of Liberal Arts."

10. *Colorado School of Mines:* The Colorado American Legion charged Frank Olmstead, a student pastor, with radicalism and demanded that he "be censored and expelled from the institution and its campus." They also urged that Mr. Ball, a trustee who encouraged Mr. Olmstead, "should be removed by the Governor as trustee and that his place . . . be filled by a patriotic citizen having the other necessary qualifications for the position, and who believes in military training . . ."

The governing board which supervised Mr. Olmstead's work asked a special independent committee of eminent citizens to investigate the charges. Their report exonerated Mr. Olmstead and included these statements:

"We deprecate, as un-American and subversive of personal liberty, the tendency of small groups of men belonging to any organization, ecclesiastical, military or political, to publish attacks upon American citizens, unsupported by competent evidence and without giving the accused any adequate opportunity to defend themselves . . .

"We do not believe that the rights of inquisition are given to any group, however patriotic in its intentions, to suppress free speech or free action in America, and to substitute their own findings for the judicial action of the Government."

The tactics of suppression in the cases cited are rather crude, so crude that the public has recognized them as what they are. They are not, therefore, the most dangerous form of this un-American development. The worst cases are those in which the methods are indirect.

For example, in a great university of the Middle West, a tactful president, instead of dismissing an instructor who objected to compulsory drill, merely reduced the instructor's teaching schedule and his salary accordingly, making it impossible for him to subsist on the remaining pittance. At another university where there was a Y. M. C. A. secretary whose opinions on the issues of race relations and the R. O. T. C. did not coincide with those of the chancellor, the chancellor recommended the discontinuance of the position instead of directly demanding the dismissal of the secretary.

Some military organizations try to make their censorship effective throughout the nation. The Reserve Officers' Associa-

18

tion, for example, (reproved by the chairman of the House Military Affairs Committee for objectionable propaganda and lobbying in its own behalf in Washington, see page 9) issued a notice which appeared in a news item from the National Secretary in the Army and Navy Journal of August 28, 1926:

> "Lt. Col. Fred B. Ryons, National Secretary of the Reserve Officers' Association of the United States, and a Nebraskan, says the 'Reserve Officer' became very much concerned over the possibility of military training in his state university being voted out. He wrote a letter to every reserve officer in the state and sent each one a copy of the Committee Hearings on the so-called 'compulsory military training bill.' With the help of the American Legion and many other citizens, the pacifists were defeated.
>
> "It is understood that the same elements back of the Nebraska fiasco expect to launch a campaign in the Southern States in November and December. If any member learns of a coming visit of a 'liberal' speaker in a school or college where there is military training, advise National Headquarters."

The section entitled "By Their Fruits" on page 22 of this pamphlet shows how the R. O. T. C. becomes involved in suppression.

E. Military Fear and Armament Competition.

Militarism is a phenomenon which has full significance only if it is studied in its international aspects. It has meaning chiefly as a philosophy which determines the attitude of one nation toward another. It is relative. When we arm, others arm; when we train, others train. And those who in other nations object to increases in their own military activities meet as their most difficult obstacle the argument that even America has taken to militarism,—and the old competition is on again.

This is clearly the case in Japan, where, the Military Intelligence Division of our War Department in commenting on the Japanese Students' Preliminary Training Act put into effect in 1926, states, "There is no doubt that the example of the Reserve Officers' Training Corps in the United States to some extent influenced the Japanese War Department." On the other hand, Premier Wakatsuke, foreign minister Shidehara, and other prominent Japanese officials publicly expressed satisfaction when they learned that President Coolidge was opposed to compulsory drill in colleges. An Associated Press dispatch from Tokyo, June 18, 1926, stated:

> "The attitude of the American president is welcome to the Tokyo government because it gives an excuse for further retrenchment in military expenditures, which is much desired by civilian officials."

Thus it is obvious that when some progress is made against militarism in America, the hands of anti-militarists are strengthened around the world. (See also reference to England, page 7.)

But in her present policy America is not very helpful to the rest of the world. Japan is not alone in being influenced by our example in the matter of military training. In India a new movement to increase the scope of military training in the colleges finds its justification in the recent development of military training in the United States.

Missionaries, who try to carry to other nations the best elements in American life, are called upon to explain why America has so greatly increased the military training of school and college boys. For example, Ira E. Gillet, in *The Christian Advocate* of October 21st, 1926, wrote: "Missionaries from America are not only concerned about the specific acts of injustice and selfishness against other peoples; we are perhaps even more alarmed at the increasing drive which the War Department is making to infect our high schools and colleges with the doctrine of force and wholesale murder under the guise of physical training and defense. We who are in a position to feel the pulse of America's neighbors know better than parents at home or students in school just how serious is the effect in these lands of a militarized education in the United States. Be quite sure that the jingo press of any other country will play up the R. O. T. C. of America quite as thoroughly to our discredit as the jingo press of America has done the military institutions of other countries."

MILITARY TRAINING AND THE MILITARY MIND-SET.

The R. O. T. C. system is deliberately used as an agency for propaganda to popularize the military. The War Department's basis for evaluation of the effectiveness of the college R. O. T. C. is given in the criteria for "Distinguished College" rating, in accordance with which inspecting officers award honors to the best college units:

"a. Support of Reserve Officers' Training Corps by the Institution.

> (1) Facilities for practical and theoretical instruction and for care of animals and equipment.
>
> (2) *Co-operation of faculty and the departments of the institution.*
>
> (3) Academic credits.

"b. *Support of Reserve Officers' Training Corps by the student body:*

(1) Enrollment in basic and advanced courses.
(2) Appointments to Officers' Reserve Corps and certificates of eligibility for such commissions.

"c. Efficiency of theoretical Reserve Officers' Training Corps instruction.

"d. Efficiency of practical Reserve Officers' Training Corps instruction."[22] (Italics supplied.)

The first two points (a and b) consider the extent to which the military establishment has succeeded in popularizing itself. Thus, if the student paper does not boost the R. O. T. C., that unit has little hope of being recognized as successful. And does not the second point under "a," mentioning the co-operation of the faculty, explain the zeal of the R. O. T. C. commandants in many institutions in suppressing discussion?

Major William W. Edwards, writing in the Infantry Journal for October, 1924, frankly stated the purpose of the R. O. T. C.:

"The Defense Act has two distinct functions. The first is so obvious as to need no comment, that of training officers and men for the reserve forces; its second function, while not less important, is less apparent, and therefore sometimes overlooked entirely, that of training the popular public mind to the necessity and needs of defense. The Junior R. O. T. C. fulfills the first mission indirectly, and for the second, I believe, there is no greater or better agency at our command. The High School boy in his Sophomore year is in his most plastic and enthusiastic stage. He is at the age of hero worship and idealism. . . ."

The Assistant Secretary of War, Colonel Hanford MacNider, explained to the National Association of Manufacturers that the Munitions Battalion would be successful in the case of the college student, "If we [the War Dept.] have taught him to think correctly about this business of ours..." Colonel MacNider said further:

"He will never forget what we have given him, if we have made him think. He will always think of industry in relation to the army's problems, just as he will think what he can do for the army if that problem is ever thrown up before him again.

"At the end of ten years, we will have 4,000 young veterans of the Munitions Battalion out in the industrial world."[16]

In view of this emphasis upon the mind-set as the fundamental aim of military training one reads with deep apprehension the following significant words from the Annual Report of the Secretary of War for the year 1926:

"During the course of a year the War Department guides, for varied periods, the lives of over 400,000 young Americans enrolled in the Regular Army, the National Guard, the Reserve Officers' Training Corps and the Citizens Military Training Camps."[23]

"BY THEIR FRUITS".

The proof that the R. O. T. C. is set up and administered in such a way as to create a militaristic mind-set is seen in the fact that it actually produces militaristic products. Scabbard and Blade is the national honorary fraternity of the R. O. T. C. Only students who attain distinction, who merit recognition because of the excellence of their R. O. T. C. work, are honored by election to membership. The army officers are usually associate members. They are, therefore, the cream of the R. O. T. C. student products. Charters for local chapters of the fraternity are granted only to institutions where the military system is active—about seventy colleges and universities at the present time.

At the National Convention of the society in 1926 the publication of a series of special situation bulletins was authorized. These Bulletins, thus authorized, and issued from the national headquarters to the chapters for the use of their members will, therefore, constitute the best and fairest basis for judging the fruits of the R. O. T. C. They cannot be attributed to an exceptional local group or to an irresponsible and uninfluential individual.

HOW THE CREAM OF THE R. O. T. C. THINKS.

The alleged purpose of the bulletins is to disseminate information about "dangerous" individuals and organizations which should be combatted because of their "subversive" work or utterances. The first issue of the bulletin states:

"It is our earnest hope that you will retain this document for future reference and publicity use, if speakers appear in your city to orate against national defense."

And again:

"Americans should be on guard against any propaganda from any source whatsoever belittling and deriding the benefits obtainable through our present R. O. T. C. and C. M. T. C. systems."

The Federal Council of Churches of Christ in America is mentioned for the publication of a pamphlet on military training. Then follows a black list of fifty-four persons with derogatory biographical sketches—the endorsers of the Lane pamphlet. (Referred to on page 7 above.)

The selection of acts, utterances, or affiliations which Scabbard and Blade considers damning reveals as in a mirror the attitude of the R. O. T. C. on public questions. Here are a few brief excerpts:

22

Jane Addams—". . . for the past twenty years her efforts have been directed to international and subversive channels until today she stands out as the most dangerous woman in America."*

William E. Borah—"R. M. Whitney in 'Reds in America' indicates connection with American Civil Liberties Union."

Henry Sloane Coffin—"The 'Lusk Report' lists him as one of a group of clergymen who signed a protest against the 'Espionage Act'."

Charles W. Gilkey—"He was one of a group of clergymen who, under date of May 22nd, petitioned the Chicago Tribune to remove Stephen Decatur's statement, 'My country right or wrong', from its editorial page stating that it bred a false kind of patriotism."

Rufus M. Jones—"He is author of a number of books, one of his last being 'The Churches' Debt to Heretics'."

William H. Kilpatrick—"He also openly opposed the Lusk Laws."

George Foster Peabody—"He is interested in negro schools, being a trustee of the American Church Institute for Negroes and the Hampton Normal and Agricultural Institute. The latter is said to be a 'hotbed' of race equality."

J. Henry Scattergood—"In an address before a 'peace luncheon' in Minneapolis, on July 20, 1924, he declared in effect that the people must drop hate and work for peace."

William E. Sweet—"In 1922 Mr. Sweet was a subscriber to the pamphlet service of the American Civil Liberties Union and also was in England studying workers' education and industrial relationships."

Abba Hillel Silver—"He is very pro-labor. 'Finance and Industry' of December, 1920, speaking of Silver stated:

'Rabbi Silver said that the open shop was an attack against unionism and that any attempt on the part of the employers to crush the unions would be resented by the general public.'"

After listing in addition to the above such persons as Prof. John Dewey, the late Francis E. Clark, Zona Gale, President Henry Noble MacCracken, Senator Norris, Rabbi Stephen S. Wise, and President Mary E. Woolley, the Bulletin states: "The biographical sketches herewith given hit only the 'high spots' in the careers of but a very small percentage of that element in our country who, possessed of constipated mentality, engaged in

*Author's note—On the occasion of a dinner in honor of Miss Addams in Chicago in January, 1927, President Coolidge sent a message of tribute in which he said, "Her work at Hull House has been a great contribution to the public welfare. It has set an example which has been an inspiration to well-doing all over the country. I trust that the testimonial of affection and regard which you are about to offer her may give her renewed strength and courage to carry on her work of peace and good will." Governor Alfred E. Smith joined in honoring her: "No American has contributed so much to awaken our social conscience. She has been a statesman of society, cooperating with public officials to make government an instrument to serve humanity." Mayor Dever of Chicago said, "She has done more to promote the real welfare of Chicago than all our political organizations."

their favorite pastime of tearing down, offer nothing constructive as an alternative for a solution of the all-embracing subject matter of national defense." Yet most of the defamatory citations describe constructive activity in behalf of tolerance and cooperation between nations, races, and classes; e. g. Miss Addams.

Since direct statements like those in the Bulletin might not always be convincing, the Bulletin instructs the young officer-censors in the use of innuendo and in the tactics of military propaganda as follows:

"Let me quote to you part of a letter received at Headquarters from an Army Officer. This quotation contains sound advice. 'As to Subversive Agitation, the important thing is to fight it without seeming to fight. Fight it with FACTS and FIGURES, with Venom and Fury, yes but CONCEAL the Venom and Fury. There is a positive advantage in: NEVER displaying animosity, NEVER showing ill-temper; and NEVER treating the other side with anything but courtesy. Always state publicly that those opposing your ideals are doubtless actuated as you are, by motives of sincerity and by the desire to work for the general welfare. But, ADD, or. let it be inferred, that these misguided Americans suffer from lack of complete information, or from errors of judgment, or from contact with radicals, communists, enemies of social order, who are deceiving them, duping them, using them as catspaws—themselves devoted to evil, to plots against our governmental system, to bolshevism but wily foes, difficult to unmask!" (The capitals are used in the original.)

We give just one example of how the Bulletin carries out this use of inference. It quotes an order from Moscow for the organization of an American branch of the "Red Sport International of Moscow", and then, without transition continues:

"The most prominent of the American organizations are:
The Pioneer Youth
The Young Workers' League of America
The Young Peoples' Socialist League (known as the Upsils)
Fellowship of Reconciliation
Fellowship of Christian Social Order
League for Industrial Democracy
Fellowship of Youth for Peace
Urban League
Woman's International League for Peace and Freedom—Department for The Youth Movement.
"These organizations are Communist-controlled, either directly or by way of interlocking directorates. There are a multitude of smaller organizations in churches, schools and colleges, such as:
International Y. M. C. A., New York City
World's Student Christian Federation, New York City
Corda Fratres Association of Cosmopolitan Clubs of America, Minneapolis, Minn.
Intercollegiate Cosmopolitan Clubs of New York City
The International Students' Assembly, New York City
Intercollegiate Press Association, Yellow Springs, Colo.
Young Woman's Christian Association

24

National Student Forum, New York City
National Student Volunteer Union, Denver, Colo.
Baptist Young People
The Congregational Young People
National Conference of Methodist Students."

We submit that a system which produces officially such material as these bulletins is militaristic in the worst sense of this word; and militarism is equally evident in the fact that R. O. T. C. students accept such material uncritically and accede to the use of such methods in the name of patriotism.

DELIBERATE WAR DEPARTMENT CAMPAIGN IN PROGRESS.

The great increase in military training in schools and colleges since the war has not resulted from a spontaneous demand by the general public or the ex-service men. It has been artificially stimulated and carefully promoted by the War Department. (To prove this is not to pronounce moral judgment upon all professional military men, even though we heartily condemn the scheme. We may respect them so long as they are fair and democratic in their methods. Nor would we impugn their motives; it is quite natural for any man to over-estimate the importance of his own profession. Those who play up the military for political, economic and selfish motives are in another category.)

During the war, of course, drill was very popular. But as soon as the war was over, the enrollment in drill fell off precipitately, while the number of students in the colleges was increasing rapidly. As long as the ex-service men were in college, the R. O. T. C. enrollment continued to decline.

Then in November, 1922, the Secretary of War called the Conference on Training for Citizenship and National Defense, to which were invited Army officers, Reserve officers, college presidents, (most of them from land-grant institutions), boys' work directors, and others. In his opening address, the secretary explained that the War Department was assuming the role of educator. He said:

> "*We are interested primarily in the on-coming generation,* for upon them certainly rests the future of our Nation, and perhaps in a larger sense than we may realize at this moment, the future of our civilization and the world . . . *The preparation of that generation is in our hands.* It is by far our most sacred charge. Even now we are molding it by what we do and what we neglect to do. Therefore, it is most fitting that those of us who are particularly charged with the care and de-

25

velopment of the youth of our Nation *in the period when mind and body and soul are being formed* should confer together for the purposes of surveying the situation and advancing well-considered plans for the development of our future citizenship."[24] (Italics supplied.)

He lamented the fact that the Federal Government could not directly control the public school system. Such being the case, the central military department could not directly superimpose a military regime on the public. As he put it:

"The War Department finds itself in a peculiar dilemma. While the Federal Government is responsible for national defense, for the raising and maintenance of armies and a navy, the physical, moral, and mental education of our youth is reserved to the states and to the people. The Federal Government finds itself with a large responsibility, but with no jurisdiction over the fundamental factors upon which success ultimately depends."[25]

Being thwarted constitutionally as regards direct action, the only recourse was through indirect methods. Since the R. O. T. C. could not be superimposed, it was necessary to "popularize" it artificially. General Pershing stated the point bluntly:

"That we have not adopted the principle of universal military service renders it highly essential that training which leads up to, and as far as possible includes preparation for military service should be popularized by all available methods."[26]

"WE MUST BE PRACTICAL IN THIS WORLD."

These methods have gradually become more "practical" with increased experience. The War Department is relying more and more on those whom it may draw in "to take the lead in making examinations and reports"; but it has not yet resigned its authority to determine what "future action" is to be taken. With naive frankness the secretary in his closing address made a most significant pronouncement:

"If the War Department had the appropriations available for the purpose [promoting the military training program] and were to undertake to do this by itself, criticism would at once be raised that we were doing it entirely for military purposes. Hence, it is necessary for you and others who may be drawn into this matter to work and even to take the lead in making examinations and reports on which future action must be based. We must be practical in this world."[27]

A letter from the War Department to all Corps Area Commanders reported by the Associated Press on December 6, 1925, is quoted as stating officially "the War Department stands squarely in favor of military training for the greatest possible number of students, considering available personnel, funds and equipment."

The assistant secretaries and the chief of staff frequently go out of their way to plead for more drill. Army officers (see page 7) and sections of the press (Boston Transcript, September 8, 1926) look upon the promotion of the R. O. T. C. as one of the chief functions, if not the chief function, of the War Department at the present time.

WHY NOT USE THE WORDING OF THE LAW?

The National Defense Act authorizes the establishing of units where the training shall be given in a "two years elective or compulsory course",[28] showing no intention of favoring compulsion. Why then does the War Department in the contract form which is signed by the college president in applying for a unit change the wording so that it reads "two years compulsory (or elective) course"?[29]

It is this latter wording which the department uses in its Bulletin describing the organization of the R. O. T. C. system and the relation of the college to the department. Why has the Department made such an important change of emphasis in the conditions drawn up by the legislators?

FALSE ANALOGY.

We hear it argued that a school or college is justified in requiring military training of all students because it requires rhetoric and mathematics. It is maintained that there is no more reason for excusing a boy from drill because he dislikes it than for excusing him from rhetoric because he dislikes composition writing. Now, we have no sympathy for the boy who objects to R. O. T. C. merely because he dislikes the exertion. He should be compelled to participate regularly in group athletics or strenuous free movement gymnastics, freed from a hot and unhygienic uniform; but we protest against compulsion in the case of the boy whose conscience or judgment dictates against the military. For compulsory drill and compulsory rhetoric are not analogous. Statutory evidence and legal practice have put them in different categories.

Objection to participation in military affairs as a matter of conscience is a legally recognized political right of the individual citizen. Conscientious objectors are excused under the National Defense Act of 1920 from combat service even during a national emergency. That military training in schools in peace-time is in principle subject to the same exemption is legally recognized in Massachusetts where the General Laws provide:

"The exercises of the Public School may include calisthenics, gymnastics, and military drill, but no pupil shall be required to take any part in any military exercises if his parent. or guardian is of any religious denomination conscientiously opposed to bearing arms, or is himself so opposed and the school committee is so notified in writing."[30]

In other states than Massachusetts, however, such a student and his parents are usually told that if they do not submit they are not entitled to the benefits of the institution which their taxes help to support. Consequently, if they are not able to meet the heavier financial requirements of a private institution, they must surrender either conscience or education, and perhaps both career and ambition. This system is so nearly "peace-time conscription" that the term is appropriately descriptive, as applied by Professor Otis. (See page 10.)

OBLIGATIONS OF LAND-GRANT COLLEGES.

No civil educational institution is under legal or moral obligation to the Federal Government to maintain military training on a compulsory basis, under the Morrill Land Grant Act of 1862, the National Defense Act, or any other federal law. The contrary statements of some military men and a few college presidents fall before the following facts and official opinions:

(1) The University of Wisconsin, a Land Grant College, abolished compulsory drill in 1922, and has suffered no diminution of federal appropriations. In connection with this case the Secretary of the Interior wrote on July 19, 1923:

"According to the Act approved July 2, 1862, it is clear that the branches of instruction, which include military tactics, are to be taught 'in such manner as the legislatures of the states may respectively prescribe' . . . Military training according to the Federal law is clearly placed in the same category as the other branches of learning which are named. Instruction in military tactics is obviously a requirement on the states as are the other branches which are mentioned. It does not appear, however, from the Federal legislation that instruction in military tactics is any more obligatory on the individual student than is instruction in agriculture or mechanic arts. The common practice of excepting third and fourth year students as well as many first and second year students for various reasons seems to be a recognition of the principle just stated."

(2) Mr. Morrill's bill providing for the granting of land to the states for the establishing and maintenance of these agricultural colleges had passed both houses of Congress in 1859,

but had been vetoed by President Buchanan. That original bill included *no reference to military tactics.*[31]

(3) When the Morrill bill was brought up in the Senate again, in war time, on May 19th, 1862, by Mr. Wade, the reference to military tactics was inserted *in parentheses.*[32] There is no indication in the debates or elsewhere that this new feature had anything to do with the new President's signing the bill.

(4) Congress made other grants of land to various states for the endowment of institutions of learning without making any reference to the state's obligation to even offer military training. Mr. Morrill's specific reference to military tactics, during war time, has no parallel in his first bill (before the war) or in acts of Congress in 1804, 1806, 1807, 1811, 1816, 1819, 1827, 1845, 1854, 1881, 1883 and 1889.

(5) In a letter to Walter C. Longstreth, on May 14, 1927, Hubert Work, Secretary of the Interior, states:

"A land-grant college, by changing its course in military training from a compulsory to an elective course, would not suffer any diminution in the appropriations that it now receives from the United States Government under any of the Acts of Congress providing aid for such institutions. . . . The University of Wisconsin did not forfeit any of the support it was receiving from the United States Government by reason of its changing its course in military training from a compulsory to an elective course."

(6) John W. Weeks, Secretary of War, on November 18, 1924, wrote to Walter C. Longstreth, saying:

"I am pleased to inform you that the National Defense Act does not make military training compulsory at any of the institutions which receive the benefits authorized by the Act. So far as the War Department is concerned it is optional with the authorities of the school, college or university whether military training shall be an elective or a compulsory course in the curriculum."

FINANCIAL AND OTHER INDUCEMENTS TO THE SCHOOL AND COLLEGE.

Where drill is compulsory, the administration is relieved of the obligation and financial burden of providing gymnasium equipment and instruction. When drill is made optional or is abolished the administration must raise a larger budget.

The armories may be used for great university convocations.

A cavalry unit and polo team are attractive advertising features of the institution's equipment. The catalogue of the Oregon State Agricultural College announces:

"The value of the Government equipment now on hand at the College is approximately a half-million dollars."

The Chicago High School R. O. T. C. cost the Federal Government $222,533.03 for one year, in addition to the initial cost of equipment, according to a report of Superintendent McAndrew.

The Cleveland School Board was blamed by some of its opponents for cutting off a source of income by abolishing the R. O. T. C. from Cleveland's high schools. The Assistant Superintendent of Schools there estimated that it would cost from $20,000 to $25,000 to make physical training available to the boys in the high schools.[33]

In Jacksonville, Florida, those who were advocating the installing of an R. O. T. C. in the city high schools called the attention of the board to the financial inducements.

But the nation pays all these bills. *So the citizens of Cleveland and Minneapolis are helping to pay the expenses of Chicago's R. O. T. C. even though they have abolished drill from their own schools.*

HOW IS THE TRAINING POPULARIZED?

A. FINANCIAL INDUCEMENTS.

39 percent of the students enrolled in 408 colleges and universities in the U. S. last year were partially or wholly self-supporting.[34] The percentage of men students alone is higher. Money-earning and money-saving schemes are therefore enticing to large numbers.

Uniforms, including overcoats suitable for everyday wear, are issued to students in the basic course. In the advanced course, in addition to clothing, cash subsistence of about $100 a year is added, with additional compensation for summer camps.

It must be remembered that the compensation is not for extra-curriculum work, but for work which is also given credit toward a degree.

At the University of Illinois, the cadet officers are paid $100 in addition to the cash subsistence; at Cornell from $75 to $250.

In the case of the Munitions Battalion, the student's college expenses for his Senior year are to be paid. He is to be recruited into the regular army at the end of his Junior year, spend his three months' summer vacation in the army, return to college for his Senior year, *with expenses paid,* and after graduation complete the remaining nine months of a year's enlistment in the

30

army. The Assistant Secretary of War explains that this should appeal to the boy who is working his way through college.

College catalogues announce the financial inducements:

University of Arkansas—"The total money value of uniform received, commutation of subsistence, rations in kind at Camp, pay at Camp, and transportation to and from Camp for each man who completes the four year course, is about $400.00."

Western Maryland College—Uniforms "and over $200 cash from the government" for advanced course.

Cornell University—"The University provides pay, ranging from $75 to $250 annually, for each of the seventy-three commissioned officers of the Reserve Officers' Training Corps. In addition, the twenty-six senior officers are assistants in the department."

B. ACADEMIC CREDIT.

The college catalogues reveal a wide variation in the amount of credit given for military work. In some cases the credit is negligible because the college authorities do not recognize the work as meriting academic reward. Others grant a B. S. degree in Military Science.

Pennsylvania State College gives 4 credits for the basic and 14 for the advanced courses.

The University of North Dakota gives 2½ credits for the first year.

C. SUMMER CAMPS.

The summer camps in most cases, especially the cruises of the Naval R. O. T. C., serve as a very pleasant vacation at the nation's expense, with an allowance of 5 cents a mile for transportation to the camp and 75 cents a day as pay while there.

D. POLITICAL AND SOCIAL ADVANTAGES.

The advanced R. O. T. C. course, in addition to giving financial remuneration with academic credit and an officer's commission, is an "activity", carrying with it social and political prestige. There are the honorary fraternities,—"Scabbard and Blade" for the military; and "Compass and Chart" for the naval, already organized at the University of Washington.

The Military Ball is the most brilliant social event of the year on many college campuses and in many high schools. Always the cadet officers shine in their natty uniforms. On social occasions, in parades, competition days, inspections, the medieval lady worshipping her protector knight is brought up to date. If there are girls on the campus each company may have its co-ed sponsor popularly elected or appointed by the captain; or the unit may elect an "honorary colonel", whose picture may appear in the papers of 21 states* from coast to coast as the best looking or the most popular girl in the high school or university. At the military ball which opens the formal social season at the University of Nebraska, "the dancers pause a moment in the midst of festivities and a spotlight is thrown on a curtain at one end of the hall. The curtain parts. The honorary colonel steps forth to lead the grand march. Cheers." Sororities may act as sponsors, in which case dances and return parties are in order.

E. "RELIGION" AND "PATRIOTISM"

Captain Ira L. Reeves, U. S. Army, in 1914 wrote an exhaustive history entitled "Military Education in the United States." The first chapter is on "Military Education, Generally." As a quotation head to this chapter, Captain Reeves used the following quotation in bold type, thus:

"The Church utters her most indignant anathema at an unrighteous war, but she has never refused to honor the faithful soldiers who fight in the cause of their country and God. The gentlest and most Christian of modern poets has used the tremendous thought:

'God's most dreaded instrument
In working out a pure intent
Is man arrayed for mutual slaughter,
Yea, Carnage is his daughter.'

—Frederick William Farrar."

The R. O. T. C. students are explicitly taught that war is in accordance with "Divine laws." (See Page 5.) Then when a Chaplain,† with the prestige of the church and the War Department, declares to the students that self-preservation is the fundamental law of life, the benediction of religion on the R. O. T. C. is supposed to be complete, and the average cadet is satisfied.

Another subtle fundamental incentive is the identification of patriotism with military service, and incidental to that, the superior patriotic prestige of the officer. This association in the case of the R. O. T. C. is strengthened and perpetuated by parades on

---

*The case of Miss Louvae Crum of Wichita (Kansas) University.
†As in the address of Chaplain C. P. Futcher at the University of Illinois, April 1, 1927.

national holidays, in which the cadets march along with the veterans. The uniform is an ever-present symbol. And this association idea of the superior patriotism of the uniformed man is unduly enhanced by the facts that the training is promoted by a branch of the United States Government and that it is supported by military-patriotic societies.

We would not diminish in the least degree the honor due to those who in a spirit of unselfish sacrifice have served their country in a military capacity when it has resorted to war. We would, on the other hand, point out the error of assuming that military service is the only patriotism, or that it is superior to the patriotism of the citizen who devotes himself during the long periods of peace to constructive effort in preserving the best elements in the nation's heritage and building up the institutions which will make war impossible.

ALLEGED EDUCATIONAL AND PHYSICAL BENEFITS OF DRILL.

In 1913, Dr. H. S. Drinker, then President of Lehigh University and President of the Society of the National Reserve Corps of America, in lauding students' summer military training camps, wrote:

" . . . It is an enormous error to consider or look on these camps as training schools simply to develop a measure of military efficiency. No man has better expressed the great value of systematic military training than Price Collier in his 'Germany and the Germans,' where he gives the German system credit for far more in the national advancement than mere military preparedness. As he well says, 'One can understand that Germany has little patience with the confused thinking which maintains that military training only makes soldiers and only incites to martial ambitions; when, on the contrary, she sees every day that it makes youths better and stronger, and produces that self-respect, self-control, and cosmopolitan sympathy which more than aught else lessens the chance of conflict' . . . "[35]

Such was the argument used in public to support drill in 1913; and such is the argument to-day,—except, perhaps, for the citation of Germany as an illustration.

But if the maintenance of military training in high schools on any basis and in colleges on a compulsory basis is defended because of alleged educational or physical benefits, its *superiority* to other methods must be established beyond question. In other words, those who object to the practice of compelling all physically fit men in the first two years of their college course to take military training are not under burden of proof to show that military training is mentally or physically injurious. *The burden of proof rests with those who support compulsion; they must show that drill is unquestionably superior* from an educational and a physical standpoint to gymnasium work, athletics, and to other training that prepares for leadership.

MILITARY AUTHORITY CHALLENGES PHYSICAL TRAINING VALUES OF DRILL.

If the case for compulsory drill is to stand on the basis of its physical value, one who is perhaps the outstanding military authority on physical training will have to be conclusively refuted by drill advocates—such an authority as the late Lieut.-Colonel Herman J. Koehler who was awarded the Distinguished Service Medal with the following citation: "For exceptionally meritorious and conspicuous service. At the beginning of the war he was placed in charge of the physical training in officers' training camps. These and also four divisional camps were personally visited by him. He personally instructed 200,000 officers and enlisted men of the new Army."

His opinion was as follows:

"The use of the musket as a means of physical development for any one, be he man or boy, is more than worthless. It is, in my opinion, positively injurious. I deny absolutely that military drill contains one worth feature which cannot be duplicated in every well-regulated gymnasium in the country to-day. A thorough physical training develops all the necessary soldierly qualities to the greatest degrees and does it without injury. If we have athletes, we shall never be without soldiers."[36]

According to a War Department statement issued the day after his death, July 1, 1927, "Following the war, Colonel Koehler's services were in demand for all summer training camps where he continued the excellent influence he had started at the original Plattsburg Camps."[37]

Add to Colonel Koehler's statement the fact that the army itself does not rely upon drill for physical development, but must also use calisthenics, and where is the justification for *compelling* a student to take drill for its physical value?

Many authorities could be cited in agreement with Colonel Koehler. For example, Professor Jesse F. Williams, head of the Department of Physical Education at Columbia University, one of the foremost authorities and authors in his field, and a member of the Educational Survey Commission of the Philippine

Islands in 1925, made a statement on April 18, 1926, for the House Committee on Military Affairs, the first three points of which were as follows:

"(1) Military drill in the colleges never has provided and in my judgment never can provide the kind of developmental activity essential in the organic development of young men. If it is conceived that health, strength, and vitality are essential conditions for war, it would appear that the most desirable training during college would be that which laid the foundations for organic and muscular development.

"(2) The common practice and constant tendency to substitute military drill for the developmental requirement of physical education mean not only a loss in potential power for military service, but a distinct handicap for the development of sources of strength for the whole of life.

"(3) Military drill fails to offer sufficient opportunities for struggle for self-testing activities, and for give and take situations, all of which are essential laboratory experiences in the development of a spirit of co-operation, loyalty and good sportsmanship."[38]

FEDERAL BUREAU OF EDUCATION CONDEMNS MILITARY TYPE OF DISCIPLINE.

A committee of thirty-three eminent educators was appointed to prepare a report on "Character Education," which was published by the Bureau of Education of the Department of the Interior in December, 1926. This is probably the most competent and impartial authority on the processes of character development that can be found. The report discusses the various school studies and school organizations, pointing out their respective contributions to character education; but it has no reference to military training. The military type of discipline, as defined by the Army, ("The Army Regulations define discipline as being an attitude characterized by willing and cheerful obedience to orders, by a scrupulous conformity to standardized procedure, and by unremitting effort in the appropriate sphere of initiative, evidenced in part by smartness of appearance and action, by cleanliness of person and neatness of dress, and by respect for superiors."[39]) is, however, discredited:

"While external control of children and youths is sometimes necessary for their own immediate welfare and the safety of society, real character develops only with development of self-control and self-direction in conformity with moral standards. . .A school organized and managed after the manner of a benevolent monarchy or oligarchy may make an excellent exhibition of a certain type of discipline. This may, however, make small contribution to the character forming power of the school community. As soon as the pupil escapes from this control by external authority, he is likely to fail because he is wanting in moral thoughtfulness and power of self-direction, or because he is in positive rebellion against the regime to which he has been subjected."[40]

35

Official State Investigating Commission Rejects Drill for Schools.

Again, if military drill is to be maintained in high schools on the strength of the value of its discipline, professional educators and impartial official investigating commissions must be conclusively refuted.

The "New Jersey Commission on Military Training in High Schools," after thorough study, reported in 1917:

"It is sometimes claimed that military training is the best agency for inculcating obedience. But if this claim is carefully considered it will be found that obedience to military authority is generally unthinking. It is often blind and superficial, not real. During actual war, men willingly undergo training because the work is definitely motivated; but when peace comes and men go into barracks, they feel that there is nothing of value in drill and there is a consequent tendency to evade its requirements. This kind of obedience has been, and may be, secured by similar school methods. It is obedience under restraint. When this is removed, laxity in discipline often follows. The discipline of the schools aims not at isolated acts of obedience under special circumstances, but at the habit of obedience to elders and persons in authority, It is a psychological fallacy to suppose that obedience to military authority, indeed, obedience exacted under any peculiar circumstances, may automatically be translated into the general habit of obedience. The same may be said of such qualities as alertness, promptness, industry, truthfulness, etc. It is by no means capable of demonstration that those who have had military training, or been subject to military discipline, are superior to other citizens in the possession of these qualities."[41]

Other Professional Educators Condemn Drill.

"What do Professors of Secondary Education think of Military Training in High Schools?" Under this title, in School and Society, for August 6, 1927, Professor George A. Coe reports a survey of professional opinion. His summary of 51 replies to his questionnaire follows:

"Are professors of secondary education favorable to military training in public high schools?
Of our respondents:
2 are positively in favor.
1 favors training in junior and senior years only.
2 are not opposed.
3 have no definite opinion.
1 is very doubtful.
1 conceives military training as a possible vocational subject.
5 would have no compulsory training.
33 would have none at all.

"Of the thirty-three who would have none at all, twenty-one hold positions in state and municipal institutions."

The *Commission on Military Training and Preparedness* of the World Federation of Education Associations, after two years of study, recommended to the 1927 convention of the Federation that the Federation condemn and oppose (1) military training for boys under 18 years of age, and (2) compulsory military training in civil educational institutions. The report of the commission is to be voted upon at the next convention of the Federation.

"DRILL HELPS MORONS"
"DEFECTIVE DELINQUENTS AT NAPONOCH COMPLIMENTED ON DRESS PARADE"

The above heading should not be considered facetious. We would not cast aspersions by odious comparison upon the students of our universities nor upon the institutions which advocate and employ this instrument of discipline. The heading is that given by the *New York Times* of December 2, 1926, to an Associated Press dispatch from Albany, which covers the annual report of the State Institution for Defective Delinquents to the State Commission of Prisons. The first paragraph of the dispatch is as follows:

"Military drill is an established practice at the New York State Institution for Defective Delinquents at Naponoch. The drill, established by the assistant superintendent, a former army officer, has become an important part of the training and has progressed to the point where the inmates, many of whom are morons, march in a 'creditable dress parade' twice a week."

Does not this report make it seem rather humorous to grant college credit toward an academic degree for such work? At the University of Wyoming, two-thirds of the first year course is drill. (See Page 11.)

Theodore Roosevelt Pointed Out "Limitations of Military Education."

Training which is valuable for defective delinquents is not necessarily valuable for all. It is easy to understand why even Theodore Roosevelt should advise his son against expecting to develop his capacity for leadership by attending a military school. He wrote his son "Ted" from the White House, January 21st, 1904, regarding the "merits of military and civil life":

"You would be so ordered about and arranged for, that you would have less independence of character than you could gain from them. You would have fewer temptations; but you would have less chance to develop the qualities which overcome temptations and show that a man has individual initiative."[42]

37

WHAT SOME GROUPS HAVE ACCOMPLISHED LOCALLY.

1. *University of Wisconsin*: In 1923 the state legislature made R. O. T. C. optional at the university.

2. *Cleveland High Schools*: In 1926 the city school board, supported by the parent teachers' association, some churches, women's clubs, labor groups, and others, voted the abolition of the R. O. T. C. from the high schools. The State Supreme Court of Ohio upheld the board's right in this action.

3. *Boston University*: R. O. T. C. was made optional in 1926 by order of President Marsh.

4. *Massachusetts, Minnesota, and Illinois*: In these states groups of citizens have organized themselves into State Committees on Militarism in Education.

5. *University of Minnesota*: State Committee on Militarism in Education sponsored bill in 1927 legislature to make R. O. T. C. optional at the university,—bill lost, 67 to 54.

6. *Ohio State University, College of the City of New York, University of Minnesota, University of Oregon, University of Oklahoma,* and others—Students have organized optional drill leagues and promoted widespread discussion.

7. *Nebraska*: State Citizens' Committee of One Hundred secured over 38,000 signatures to legislative petition for a referendum on compulsory R. O. T. C. at the state university.

8. *Pomona College, California*: Student protest was instrumental in bringing about the abolition of the compulsory feature of drill.

WHAT YOU CAN DO.

1. Insist that this public issue be discussed in public,—in your church, press, women's club, labor organization, public forum, etc., etc.

2. If your local high school has military training take the matter up with the school board.

3. As a tax-paying citizen, demand that the administration of your state college and university abolish the compulsory feature.

4. If there is compulsory drill in any college under your church denomination, protest to the president and trustees of that college.

5. Actively support any measure in your state legislature or in Congress (such as the "Welsh Bill," H. R. 8538) intended to abolish compulsory drill from civil colleges.

6. Unite with others in your community and state for the purpose of mobilizing public opinion against militarism in education in your state.

7. Give this pamphlet wide circulation.

8. Send at least a dollar to the Committee on Militarism in Education, 387 Bible House, Astor Place, New York City, and consult them as to how you can help further this campaign. The officers of the Committee are George A. Coe, Chairman; Rev. John Nevin Sayre and Wilbur K. Thomas, Vice-Chairmen; Rev. Thomas Guthrie Speers, Treasurer; and Roswell P. Barnes, Executive Secretary. The Executive Committee is composed of the officers and Leslie Blanchard, Eleanor Brannan, Inez Cavert, Rev. Samuel McCrea Cavert, Mrs. Charles Noel Edge, William B. Harvey, George M. LaMonte, Rev. John Herring, Halford Luccock, Patrick Malin, Frank Olmstead, Kirby Page, Norman Thomas, Henry P. Van Dusen and Kenneth Walser.

The objectives of the Committee are the following:

A. *To oppose*:

1. Compulsory military training in civil educational institutions.
2. All formal military training in high schools.
3. Federal subsidy and War Department control of military training in public schools and universities.

B. *To advocate*:

1. Free speech for peace.
2. Truth and fairness in the teaching of history.
3. School and university instruction in the causes of war and the methods of international cooperation.

ORGANIZATIONS OPPOSING COMPULSORY MILITARY TRAINING.

National

American Federation of Labor
American Friends' Service Committee
Chicago Speakers' Conference
Conference of Pacifist Churches
Disciples of Christ
Federal Council of Churches
Federation of Women's Boards of Foreign Missions of North America
General Assembly of the Presbyterian Church
International Woman's Trade Union League
Methodist Young Peoples Convention

National Council of the Congregational Church
National Council of Jewish Women
National Education Association
National Federation of Temple Sisterhoods
National Student Council of Y. M. C. A.
National Study Conference of the Churches and World Peace
Ninety-Seventh Synod of the Reformed Presbyterian Church of North
America
Northern Baptist Convention
Rabbinical Assembly of the Jewish Theological Seminary of America
Society for the Advancement of Judaism
Women's International League for Peace and Freedom
World Alliance for International Friendship Through the Churches

State

Colorado Conference of the Methodist Episcopal Church
Executive Committee of the Massachusetts Federation of Churches
Iowa Missionary Conference
Iowa State Student Council of the Y. M. C. A.
Maine Methodist Conference
Massachusetts Congregational Conference
Massachusetts High School Principals (Vote 150-9)
Ministers of the Church of Christ of Iowa
Nebraska Baptist Pastors' Conference
Nebraska Church of the Disciples
Nebraska Congregational Church
Nebraska Methodist Church
Nebraska Trade Unions
Nebraska Women's Christian Temperance Union
New Hampshire Conference of Congregational Churches
Ohio Pastors' Association Meeting
Oregon Yearly Meeting of Friends Church
Pennsylvania Federation of Churches
Pennsylvania Federation of Labor
Presbyterian Synod of New York
Presbyterian Synod of Oregon
South Dakota Conference of Congregational Churches
Wyoming Congregational Conference
Wyoming Federation of Labor

Miscellaneous

Beresford Ministerial Association of South Dakota
Congregational Ministers of Detroit
Connecticut Valley Collegiate World Court Conference
Detroit Conference of Methodist Episcopal Churches
Dunkard Students (Church of the Brethren)
Estes Park Conference of Y. M. C. A. and Y. W. C. A.
Greater Boston Federation of Churches
Indianapolis Monthly Meeting of Friends
Interstate Student Conference, Hood College
Methodist Pastors of Lincoln and Beatrice Districts
Ministerial Association of the Reformed Church of Baltimore
New York East Conference of Methodist Episcopal Church
New York, New Haven and Hartford Railroad Clerks
North East Ohio Conference of Methodist Episcopal Churches
Pastors of Eastern Conference of the Southern Nebraska District of
Missouri, Synod of Lutheran Churches

Rock River (Ill.) Conference of the Methodist Episcopal Church
Southern California Congregational Conference
Student Conference of Y. M. C. A. and Y. W. C. A. in Middle-Atlantic
States
United Parents' Association of New York City

278 AMERICAN SCHOOLS AND COLLEGES GIVE GOVERNMENT-SUPPORTED MILITARY TRAINING.*

R. O. T. C.'s, wholly subsidized by Federal Government:

Senior
    Colleges and Universities 130

Junior
    High Schools (count by cities)† 53
    Junior Colleges and Normal Schools 7
    Military Schools 38

    Total R. O. T. C. Institutions .... · 228
    (Training wholly government-subsidized.)

Federal Government-Aided Military Training:
    Under Section 55c, National Defense Act
    High Schools 15
    Junior Colleges, Normal Schools and
        Private Schools 25
    Military Academies 7
    Under Section 1225, Revised Statutes 3

    Total Government-Aided Institutions 50
    (Training partly government-subsidized.)

    Grand Total 278

*The statistics given here and on Page 9, do not include the large
number of schools where military training is given independent
of the War Department, e.g., in Massachusetts military training
is given in 23 high schools, but only 3 are included in these lists.
†This count is by cities; thus Chicago is counted once, though it
has R. O. T. C. units in 20 schools.

> "Washington, June 15th, (1926)—President Coo-
> lidge is opposed to compulsory military training for
> school or college students and to anything even that
> stimulates a military spirit in the youth of the land."
> —*New York Times*, June 16, 1926.

UNIVERSITIES AND COLLEGES WHERE MILITARY TRAINING IS COMPULSORY.

Recent catalogues show that in the following 86 colleges and universities R. O. T. C. is compulsory for at least the first two years:

UNIVERSITIES.

Cornell Univ.
Creighton Univ., (Omaha, Neb.)
DePauw Univ. (Greencastle, Ind.)
Emory Univ., (Atlanta, Ga.)
Georgetown Univ. & Medical
  School (Washington, D. C.)
Howard Univ., (Washington, D. C.)
Indiana Univ.
Lehigh Univ., (Bethlehem, Pa.)
Louisiana State Univ.
Municipal Univ. of Akron
New York Univ.
Ohio State Univ.
Pennsylvania State College
Purdue Univ., (Lafayette, Ind.)
Rutgers Univ., (New Brunswick,
  N. J.)
State Univ. of Iowa
U. of Alabama
U. of Arizona
U. of Arkansas
U. of California
U. of California, Southern Branch
U. of Dayton, (Ohio)
U. of Delaware

U. of Florida
U. of Georgia
U. of Hawaii
U. of Idaho
U. of Illinois
U. of Kentucky
U. of Maine
U. of Maryland
U. of Minnesota
U. of Missouri
U. of Montana
U. of Nebraska
U. of Nevada
U. of New Hampshire
U. of North Dakota
U. of Oklahoma
U. of Oregon
U. of Porto Rico
U. of South Dakota
U. of Tennessee
U. of Vermont & State Agr. College
U. of Washington
U. of Wyoming
West Virginia Univ.
Wilberforce Univ., (Ohio)

COLLEGES AND TECHNICAL SCHOOLS.

Agricultural College of Utah
Alabama Polytechnic Inst.
California Inst. of Technology
Coe College, (Cedar Rapids, Iowa)
Colorado Agricultural College
Colorado School of Mines
Connecticut Agr. College
Davidson College, (Davidson,
  N. C.)
Drexel Institute, (Philadelphia,
  Pa.)
Georgia School of Technology
Iowa State College
Kansas State Agr. College
Massachusetts Agr. College
Massachusetts Inst. of Technology
Michigan State College of Agr.
  & Applied Science
Mississippi Agr. & Mech. College

Missouri State School of Mines
Montana State College of Agr.
  & Mech. Arts
New Mexico College of Agr. &
  Mech. Arts
North Carolina State College of
  Agr. & Engineering
North Dakota Agr. College
Oklahoma A. & M. College
Oregon Agr. College
Presbyterian College of So. Carolina,
  (Clinton, S. C.)
Rhode Island State College
Rose Polytechnic Institute,
  (Terre Haute, Ind.)
South Dakota State College
State College of Washington
U. of Cincinnati (School of Engineering)
Western Maryland

MILITARY COLLEGES.

"Colleges and universities (including land-grant institutions) granting degrees, where the students are habitually in uniform and constantly under military discipline, and the average age on graduation is not less than 21, and where one of the leading objects is to develop students by means of military training."

Agricultural and Mech. Col. of Texas
The Citadel, Charleston, S. C.
Clemson Agricultural Col., S. C.
North Georgia Agr. College, Dahlonega, Ga.
Norwich Univ., Northfield, Vermont
Penna. Mil. College, Chester, Pa.
Virginia Agr. and Mech. Col. and Polytechnic Inst., Blacksburg, Va.
Virginia Military Institute, Lexington, Va.

UNIVERSITIES AND COLLEGES WHERE MILITARY TRAINING IS ELECTIVE.

In these 44 colleges and universities military training is
·elective:

UNIVERSITIES.

Baylor, Dallas, Texas
Boston Univ.
Col. of the City of New York
Denison, Granville, O.
Fordham Univ.
Harvard
Johns Hopkins
Leland Stanford, Jr.
Northwestern Univ., Evanston, Ill.
Princeton
.Syracuse
U. of Buffalo
U. of Chicago
U. of Kansas
U. of Michigan
U. of Pennsylvania
U. of Pittsburgh
U. of Utah
U. of Wisconsin
Washington, (St. Louis, Mo.)
Western Reserve, (Cleveland. O.)
Yale

COLLEGES AND TECHNICAL SCHOOLS.

Albany Medical College
Carnegie Institute of Technology
Cornell Univ. Medical Col., N. Y. City.
George Washington Univ. Medical School
Gettysburg Col., Penna.
Harvard Medical School, Boston
Jefferson Medical Col., Phila.
Knox, Galesburg, Ill.
Lafayette, Easton, Penna.
Medical Col. of Virginia, Richmond
Municipal Univ. of Wichita, Kans.
North Pacific Col. of Oregon
School of Dentistry, Portland, Oregon
Northwestern Univ. Dental School, Chicago
Ouachita Col., Arkadelphia, Ark .
Pomona Col., Claremont, Calif.
Ripon Col., Wisconsin
Rush Medical School, Chicago
St. Louis Univ. School of Medicine
U. of California Medical School
U. of Oregon Medical School
Vanderbilt Univ., School of Medicine, Nashville
Wofford Col., Spartanburg, S. C.

43

JUNIOR COLLEGES, NORMAL SCHOOLS, ETC., HAVING JR. R. O. T. C. UNITS.

Academy of Richmond County, Augusta, Ga.
Emory University Academy, Oxford, Ga.
Western Kentucky State Normal School, Bowling Green, Ky.
Campion College, Prairie du Chien, Wisconsin
St. Thomas Military Academy, St. Paul, Minn.
Loyola College, Los Angeles, Calif.
Punahou Academy, Honolulu

53 CITIES IN WHICH THERE ARE HIGH SCHOOLS WITH RESERVE OFFICERS' TRAINING CORPS.

20 Compulsory*

Athens, Ga.
Canon City, Colo.
Chattanooga, Tenn.
Cheyenne, Wyo.
Council Bluffs, Iowa
Gloucester, Mass.
Griffin, Ga.
Honolulu, Hawaii
Knoxville, Tenn.
Louisville, Ky.
Macon, Ga.
Memphis, Tenn.
Nashville, Tenn.
Ogden, Utah
Owensboro, Ky.
Salt Lake City, Utah
San Diego, Calif.
Santa Barbara, Calif.
St. Joseph, Mo.
Walla Walla, Washington

33 Elective

Alameda, Calif.
Atlanta, Ga.
Bangor, Me.
Beloit, Wis.
Birmingham, Ala.
Boise, Idaho
Calumet, Mich.
Chicago, Ill.
Dallas, Texas
Davenport, Iowa
Detroit, Mich.
El Paso, Texas
Fort Worth, Texas
Gary, Ind.
Grand Rapids, Mich.
Indianapolis, Ind.
Joliet, Ill.
Joplin, Mo.
Kansas City, Mo.
Leavenworth, Kan.
Long Beach, Calif.
Los Angeles, Calif.
Montgomery, Ala.
New Bedford, Mass.
Oakland, Calif.
Pasadena, Calif.
Reno, Nevada
Riverside, Calif.
Rockford, Ill.
San Antonio, Texas
San Francisco, Calif.
St. Paul, Minn.
Waukegan, Ill.

*This list is compiled from the last available reports of Superintendents of Public Instruction, high school principals, etc.

SCHOOLS HAVING MILITARY TRAINING (not R. O. T. C.) RECEIVING EQUIPMENT AND AID FROM FEDERAL GOVERNMENT.

High Schools:
Columbus Public Schools, Columbus, Ohio
Denver High Schools, Denver, Colorado
DeWitt Clinton High School, New York City
Hamilton High School, Hamilton, Ohio
John Marshall High School, Richmond, Va.
Park City High School, Park City, Utah
Phoenix Union High School, Phoenix, Arizona
Sacramento High School, Sacramento, Calif.
Sperry High School, Sperry, Oklahoma
Tucson High School, Tucson, Arizona
Wakefield High School, Wakefield, Mass.
Washington High Schools, Washington, D. C.
Washington High Schools (Colored), Washington, D. C.
Winchester High School, Winchester, Va.
Xavier High School, New York City

Junior Colleges, Normal Schools, Private Military Schools, etc.:
Albany Academy, Albany, New York
Bailey Military Institute, Greenwood, S. C.
Baylor School, Chattanooga, Tenn.
The Benedictine School, Savannah, Ga.
California Polytechnic School, San Luis Obispo, Calif.
The Childrens' Village, Dobbs Ferry, N. Y.
Concordia College, Fort Wayne, Ind.
Girard College, Philadelphia, Penna.
Glenwood Manual Training School, Glenwood, Ill.
Greenbrier Presbyterian Military School, Lewisburg, W. Va.
Hargrave Military Academy, Chatham, Va.
Hill Military Academy, Portland, Oregon
John Tarleton Agr. College, Stephenville, Texas
Kansas Vocational College, Topeka, Kans.
Kentucky Military Institute, Lyndon, Ky.
Lincoln University, Jefferson City, Mo.
Linsly Institute, Wheeling, W. Va.
Locust Grove Institute, Locust Grove, Ga.
McCallie School, Chattanooga, Tenn.
Marist College, Atlanta, Ga.
Maryland Training School for Boys, Lock Raven, Maryland
Miami Military Institute, Germantown, Ohio
Negro Agr. and Tech. College, Greensboro, N .C.
North Texas Agric. College, Arlington, Texas
Prairie View State Normal and Industrial College, Prairie View, Texas
The Principia, St. Louis, Mo.
St. Emma Industrial and Agric. Institute, Rock Castle, Va.
St. John's College, Washington, D. C.
San Diego Army and Navy Academy, Pacific Beach, Calif.
San Marcos Academy, San Marcos, Texas
Sewanee Military Academy, Sewanee, Tenn.
State College for Colored Students, Dover, Delaware
Tuskegee Institute, Tuskegee, Ala.
Wenonah Military Academy, Wenonah, N. J.
Western University, Kansas City, Kansas

ABBREVIATED BIBLIOGRAPHY ON R. O. T. C.

(Items marked with an asterisk can be obtained through the Committee on Militarism in Education, 387 Bible House, Astor Place, New York City.)

GENERAL:

Military Training, Compulsory in Schools and Colleges, 161 pages, H. W. Wilson Co., New York, 1926.

Brig. Gen. John McC. Palmer—*"Statesmanship or War"*, Doubleday, Page and Co., 1927.

FOR R. O. T. C.

J. A. Kenderdine—*"The Other Side of Military Training"*, *The Survey*, January 13, 1926.

Brig. Gen. L. R. Gignilliat—"Students and National Defense"*, *World Tomorrow*, October, 1926.

P. S. Bond—*"Our Military Policy"*, 63 pages, published by *The Military Engineer*, Mills Bldg., Washington, D. C., 1925.

Paul V. McNutt—*"The Menacing Gesture of Pacifism"*, *The National Republic*, May, 1927.

AGAINST R. O. T. C.

W. D. Lane—"Military Training in Schools and Colleges of the United States"*, 31 pages, March, 1926.

Lawrence G. Brooks, et al—"Military Training in the Schools and Colleges of Massachusetts,* 19 pages.

Committee on Militarism in Education—News Letters.

President Daniel L. Marsh—"What a University President Thinks of Compulsory Military Training"*, 4 pages, 1926.

World Tomorrow—Militarism in the U. S. A., issue of October, 1926.

A Progressive Militarist, *A Modest Proposal,* Atlantic Monthly, January, 1927.

Carlton J. H. Hayes—*"Essays on Nationalism"*, 279 pages, Macmillan and Co., 1926.

George A. Coe—"Shifting the National Mind-Set"*.

Winston Churchill—"Shall We Commit Suicide."*

Kirby Page—"War, Its Causes, Consequences and Cure"*, 89 pages, George H. Doran Co., New York, 1923.

Sherwood Eddy and Kirby Page—"The Abolition of War"*, 94 pages, George H. Doran Co., New York, 1924.

Representative American Opinions, 28 pages, 1926.

REFERENCES.

[1]*Militarism in our Educational Institutions—The Menace of the Junior Cadet Corps and the O. T. C.*, By Rennie Smith, B. Sc., M.P., Page 8.

[2]Navy Department and Naval Service Appropriation Bill, Fiscal Year, 1927, House of Representatives, Report of the Committee on Appropriations, Report No. 84, Page 7.

[3]Hearings before the Sub-Committee of House Committee on Appropriation Bill for 1927, Page 432.

[4]Captain Michael J. Lenihan, quoted in *"Military Education in the United States"* by Ira L. Reeves, Page 87.

[5]Report of the Secretary of War, 1925, Pages 4-9.

[6]Army List and Directory, December, 1913.

[7]Army List and Directory, January, 1927.

[8]Report of the Secretary of War to the President, 1914.

[9]War Department Notes of October 15, 1926.

[10]Report of the Secretary of War to the President, 1916.

[11]War Department Notes of December 27, 1926.

[12]World Almanac, 1927, Pages 314-315.

[13]Report of Adjutant General to the Secretary of War, 1920, Page 25.

[14]Hearings before the Committee on Military Affairs, House of Representatives, 69th Congress on H.R. 8538, Page 31.

[15]*Washington Post*, October 24, 1926.

[16]Address of Colonel Hanford McNider before the National Association of Manufacturers, Astor Hotel, New York, October 7, 1926.

[17]Army Regulations, No. 145-10, Page 1.

[18]From *"Student Military Training"*, an address by the Hon. John W. Weeks, Secretary of War, presented October 8, 1921, by Major General James G. Harboard, on behalf of the Secretary of War, Page 12.

[19]*"Manual of Military Training"* by Moss and Lang, Volume I, Fourth Revised Edition, Appendix I, Page 26.

[20]Ibid. Chapter XXVII, Page 1.

[21]*"Shifting the National Mind-Set"*, World Tomorrow, February, 1924.

[22]Army Regulations, 145-10, Page 24.

[23]Report of the Secretary of War for 1926, Page 22.

[24]Special Report of the Secretary of War to the President on The Conference on Training for Citizenship and National Defense, 1922, Page 3.

[25]Ibid., Page 6. [26]Ibid., Page 9. [27]Ibid., Page 32.

[28]National Defense Act, Section 40.

[29]Army Regulations 145-10, Page 30.

[30]Mass. General Laws, Chapter 71, Section 3.

[31]The Congressional Globe, 35th Congress, February 1, 1859, Page 713.

[32]Congressional Globe, 37th Congress, May 19, 1862, Page 2187.

[33]*Cleveland Plain Dealer*, January 17, 1926.

[34]Bureau of Education, Dept. of Interior, reported U. S. Daily. July 1, 1927, Page 1.

[35]*New York Times*, August 17, 1913.

[36]The Reference Shelf, Military Training Compulsory in Schools and Colleges. H. W. Wilson Company, Page 51.

[37]War Department Notes, July 2, 1927.

[38]Hearings before the Committee on Military Affairs, House of Representatives, 69th Congress on H.R. 8538, Page 61.

[39]"Basic Military Training"—U. S. Infantry Ass'n. Intro. Page XV.

[40]*Character Education*—Bureau of Education Bulletin, Department of the Interior, (1926)—No. 7, Page 28.

[41]The Reference Shelf, Page 47. (See item 36 above.)

[42]Theodore Roosevelt—"Letters to His Children", Page 87.

SO THIS IS WAR!

A Study of "Popularized" Military Training

by

TUCKER P. SMITH

Executive Secretary, Committee on Militarism in Education

THE LADY COLONEL

"Miss Evelyn Hoskins ... chosen as the most popular co-ed of the University of Tennessee, the award carrying with it the title of colonel in the R.O.T.C. regiment"... "Attired in full military regalia she is in the reviewing stand at every weekly dress parade."

Fotograms.

Greenwood (S. C.) *Index-Journal.* 2/5/28 *Centralia* (Washington) *Chronicle,* and scores of other papers that come to hand.

Bold face and Italics are ours throughout the pamphlet, unless **otherwise noted.**

POPULARIZING THE R. O. T. C.

In November, 1922, the Secretary of War called to Washington for a conference educators, social workers, and others dealing with youth, as well as a number of army officers, to discuss how the War Department might play its new role of breaking into the Colleges and High Schools of the country. Since this was to be a distinct innovation in America and is quite contrary to our practices and traditions—the control of schools being strictly reserved for local jurisdiction in this country—, unusual measures would be necessary if our military arm was to play any part in our educational system.

General Pershing stated the situation and suggested the way out.

> "That we have not adopted the principle of universal military service renders it highly essential that training which leads up to, and as far as possible includes preparation for military service should be popularized by all available methods."

That was in 1922. Let us examine the ways in which the training is being popularized.

POPULARIZER No. 1 — PRETTY GIRL OFFICERS AND SPONSORS.

The prettiest and most popular girls in High Schools and Colleges are selected to be honorary officers or cadet sponsors. These positions are made so attractive that normal girls are delighted thus to popularize with their beauty, preparedness for success in battle.

Newspapers all over the country carry hundreds of pictures of these girl officers "all dolled up," adding such captions as: "She's in the Army Now," "Cadets Salute Her," "Beautiful Coed Rules Ranks of Men," "Who Wouldn't Take Orders from Her," etc., etc.

DO YOU WONDER THAT GIRLS FALL FOR SUCH PUBLICITY?*

"NIFTY COLONEL. The best looking Colonel in the Country! University of S. Dak. students call Miss Eva Jean Leslie. She's honorary Colonel of the R. O. T. C. at the University, and in this capacity leads the grand march at the school's annual military ball."

> *Montgomery* (Ala.) *Journal,* 3/10/27 and 86 other papers from 30 states.

"OH, IT'S GREAT TO BE A SOLDIER when the officers are as nice looking as El Delle Johnson, 19-year-old Oldsburg, Kansas, girl. Miss Johnson has been made honorary Colonel of the Kansas State Agricultural School R. O. T. C."

> *Schenectady* (N. Y.) *Gazette. Camden* (N. J.) *Courier,* 4/21/28. etc., etc.

* Quotations are taken from beneath press clippings with photographs of the girls mentioned, showing them in different styles of military uniforms.

"ACCORDING TO MODERN TRAINING IDEAS"

"Four girls have been elected officers in the R. O. T. C. of the New Bedford High School and their commissions have been authorized by the War Department. . . . The girl officer, according to modern training ideas, furnishes a liaison between the social and military life of the school. The girl officer is expected to call the attention of the boy in training to the fact that a button may be missing on his tunic or that a grease spot may have appeared at his elbow. The reserve officer, it is believed, would more readily accept criticism from a girl than he would from a boy, and be more anxious to avoid it. The same idea prompts the training-officer to have the girl-officers accompany them on tours of inspection. . . . The 'lady officers' are known as sponsors and are elected by the student body. Thus the most popular girls in the school are officially recognized in the army organization."

Boston Post, quoted in Congressional Record for 1/4/29, p. 1166.

"The custom of appointing leading coeds as sponsors of the local Syracuse University unit of the R. O. T. C. was established two years ago to further favorable sentiment towards the unit among the student body. It is considered one of the highest honors that a Syracuse woman may receive."

Binghamton (N. Y.) *Press,* 11/20/28.

"THE HARD-BOILED LITTLE COLONEL"

"Colonel——student at university——female Colonel . . . . . youngest student . . . only fourteen . . . is and has been for some time honorary commanding officer of the R. O. T. C. at —— The Corps, from Cadets to Major, is maintained by the War Department, and Colonel——is the ranking officer . . . rules regiment with iron hand . . . known as 'the hard-boiled little Colonel'."

"Little Colonel——in uniform and with a sword, which she wears with grace, directs all parades, reviews, drills, inspections; and, when, each year the regiment holds its military ball she doffs her soldierly garb for more feminine attire, and presides on that occasion as 'Queen of the Ball'."

"She takes just as much interest in her outfit as if her entire career depended upon it. 'If there were a war', she stoutly insists, 'I'd go to the scene of action with my outfit, and I'd lead them into battle. I've studied every military campaign from Hannibal to Pershing, and I know the soldiering trade. If Joan of Arc could lead an army into battle, why couldn't I lead a regiment?' "

Story and photographs in Boston Advertiser, Boston Globe, Detroit Times, etc.

[4]

"ALWAYS FILLED are the ranks of the Reserve Officers' Training Corps at Ogden High School, Ogden, Utah. The photo above is the reason. These girls are sponsors of the organization who have been equipped with special uniforms to help them carry out their duties."

Central Press Photo. *Elizabeth* (N. J.)*Journal*, 11/26/28.

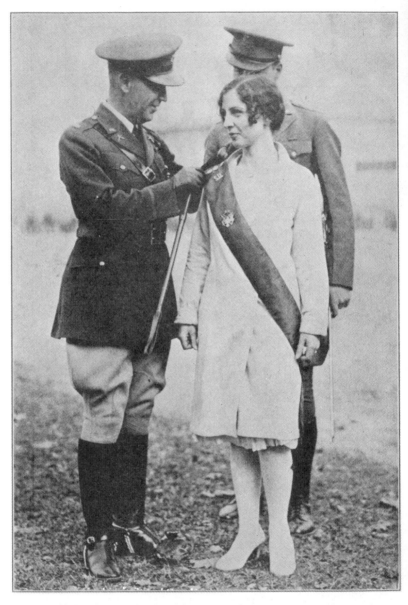

"While the student soldiers stood at attention, Maj. George S. Clark, commandant, pinned the insignias of rank on the sponsors. He is shown giving Miss Mary O'Reilly her captain's bars."

By permission, *Syracuse* (**N. Y.**) *Journal*, 11/2/28.

"ONE REASON FOR OUR WELL DRESSED STUDENT ARMY"

"Probably the most popular officers who ever scrutinized a rank of rookies are these four commissioned officers of New Bedford, Mass. (High School) R.O.T.C. Colonel Harry P. Wilbur, Commandant of the Unit, decided the men of his outfit would take more pride in their appearance if they knew they were to be inspected regularly by the best looking girls in the High School. These honorary commissions are the result."   Acme.

Ironton Tribune (Ohio), 11/23/26. *Danville Press* (Ill.) etc., etc.

"The sponsor idea is a new one in Indianapolis High Schools . . . Their duties . . . . are 'to participate in all ceremonies of the battalion, to build up interest in the reserve training corps of the high school, . . . to inspect their companies each Friday for cleanliness, neatness of uniform, belt, shoes, appearance'. The battalion sponsor assumes charge of the company sponsors."

Indianapolis News, 11/8/28.

"In these days rulers cannot make war without the consent of the ruled. Formerly, Kings and Princes could wage war on each other with small professional armies. But the days of the small professional army have gone forever. Whole nations now fight, and if the people are not willing, war is impossible. The trouble is that too many of the people themselves are still too willing. This is partly the valour of ignorance. Centuries of propaganda for war have borne their fruit. The romantic side of war looms large to those who have not experienced its horrors or witnessed its bestialities."

Lt. Commander J. M. Kenworthy in "Peace or War", p. 25. Boni & Liveright.

[7]

"COED TAKES MILITARY HONORS"

"Seattle, July 14. Miss Alyce Wester, first co-ed of the once wild-west to take reserve officers' training camp drill has been made a Colonel in the R.O.T.C. at the University of Washington here. The honor comes after a year of training with members of the corps on the campus.

"Miss Wester, 20-year old junior in the college of liberal arts, is studying infantry drill, musketry, and automatic rifle shooting.

"In addition she is a two year veteran on the rifle team.

" 'Rifle shooting is my hobby,' she said. 'I want to study its practical application to warfare. That's why I joined the R. O. T. C.' "

Central Press Photo.
Reading (Pa.) Eagle, 7/15/28.

MISS R. O. T. C.

"Stillwater, Oklahoma, Oct. 14. (Special)—Forty-nine co-eds at the Oklahoma Agricultural and Mechanical College have enrolled in the reserve officers' training corps for military training. Rifle marksmanship, military tactics, and army ethics will be included in the course. Photograph shows Miss Roberta Sanborn, of Stillwater, taking her first lesson in marksmanship."

Oklahoma City Oklahoman, 10/15/27.

"ADMITS 'IT' IS USED TO AID R.O.T.C. IDEA"

"Girl Sponsor Agrees Sex Appeal Is Capitalized On Behalf of Students."

"Charges made in the House of Representatives by Representative Ross A. Collins, Democrat, Mississippi, that sex appeal and social aspirations are capitalized in the nation-wide development of the military idea were declared true last night by the regimental sponsor of the Reserve Officers' Training Corps at the University of Maryland.

"Miss Estelle Nickell, of Rising Sun, Md., who was chosen early in November as sponsor of the R.O.T.C. regiment at the university, said:

" 'It is true' . . . . .

"The fact that the boys like to have girls watch them sometimes at the drills would probably account for the popularity of the practice. And it does undoubtedly add to the amount of publicity that can be given the R.O.T.C. . . . ."

Pictures are Published.

"This year, shortly after the sponsors were chosen, the pictures of the sponsors were published in the college paper. This is publicity for the R.O.T.C., and also for the girls . . . .

"Miss Leighton added that she thought the sponsors were instrumental in getting more students to take the advanced course in military training, which is optional at the university.

" 'While there is no doubt that the sponsors do have their advertising value', she added, 'the practice should not be condemned because of that. It has its own value. There is no doubt it instills some dignity in the troop maneuvers and in such wise is of material assistance to the school' " . . . . .

Termed an Honor.

" 'We have no duties,' Miss Laughlin said. 'We just are supposed to be present at all of the reviews and inspection. We parade around with the officers and walk with them during inspection and look over the troops' . . .

" 'It is quite an honor,' she added. 'It is one of the biggest honors a girl can get.' "

Baltimore Sun, 1/7/29.

"MONKEY BUSINESS"

"There are a legion of expedients for making instruction in' teresting . . . "

"There is one thing, however, to guard against. The 'interest' feature can be stressed to such a degree that all the professional military value of the instruction is lost" . . .

"Such 'instruction' wins no wars" . . .

"We are all necessarily specialists in this business of making war, and a wise policy would require each to stick to his specialty."

. . ."Reservists, along with the rest of us, dote on diversion, and if they can find diversion which their consciences will accept as military instruction, they will play that kind of game indefinitely."

. . . "it has no other value whatever unless it be the very nebulous one of 'keeping alive the military fraternity' in the vicinity. Why the military fraternity should be kept alive under such circumstances requires some explanation."

Major H. A. Finch, Corps of Engineers,
In the Infantry Journal June, 1927.

"WAR DEPARTMENT DECLARES IT HAS NOTHING TO DO WITH APPOINTING GIRLS"

... "The War Department not only has nothing to do with choosing of the sponsors but also is not even informed as to their identity and number.

... "When the inspectors come from the War Department they don't ask about the sponsors," he continued. "They don't care anything about them, as they are not part of the military organization of the corps. They have and receive no military training and are not supposed to have any. **They do not wear uniforms.**"

Baltimore Sun, 11/7/29.

This statement given to a reporter at the time of the controversy on the floor of the House over "popularizing" the R.O.T.C. is rather typical of the attitude of the officials of the War Department. When challenged they disclaim responsibility for the actions of their representatives stationed over the country, though those officers appear in uniform and speak as officers.

However, the responsibility of the War Department for this popularizing program is shown in a number of ways:

1. The conference mentioned on page three.

2. In the quotation below which is taken from a detailed plan for establishing military training in the public schools and for making it popular there, printed in the report of the Secretary of War for 1916.

3. **In the fact that the support given a cadet corps by the college authorities and its popularity with the student body are large factors in determining whether a particular college will be given distinguished rating when inspected by officers from headquarters. Sponsors serve this very purpose.**

4. Just look at the picture on the opposite page, and then turn to page 6 where a regular army officer seems to be "taking notice of" a girl sponsor.

"Plan for Military Training in Public Schools of the United States."

"Sponsors are elected from the girls in the mixed schools and assigned to competition units. The sponsors are in every sense members of the cadet organization. They attend all drills, are the leaders in all social affairs, and while they do not actually drill, the sponsors are entitled to receive such individual rewards as may be won by their units.

"Medals, ribbons and distinctive marks on the uniform are given each member of a winning unit, the sponsor of course, included."

From the report of the Chief of Staff of the Army for 1916.

"LET'S ALL PRESENT ARMS!"

" 'With so pretty a Colonel, it is no wonder the Creighton
R.O.T.C. is such a well-drilled unit' said Major General Charles
P. Summerall, Chief of Staff of the United States Army, as he re-
viewed the cadets at the Omaha School."
By permission, *Omaha Bee-News,* 11/27/28.

·POPULARIZER No. 2—GIRL RIFLE TEAMS.

A college sport that is easy to coach, delightful to practice, a joy to root for,—and what a banquet you can give the winning team! While Uncle Sam helps pay the bills.

The University of Kansas Girls' Rifle Team fired against thirty-six teams from institutions all over the country.   P & A Photo.

"Members of the girls' rifle corps at a Los Angeles High School, who have invaded the rifle range of the R. O. T. C. and practice there with regulation guns."—International Photo.

New Orleans Times Picayune, 11/20/27.

"ONE OF THE REASONS"

"for the success of the women's rifle team of George Washington University is Helen Taylor, the Captain."—Acme Photo.

N. Y. Telegram, 11/16/28.

"**The girls have rifle teams, and they like it;** and, of course, it does not cost them anything. **It helps to make them popular, and they join in the game.** So many of these training units are so well supplied with officers and men that they have time to coach these teams on the side—as a delight to themselves, to the girls, and to the community. **The press is filled with pictures of these fair marksmen** . . . **The fact that these news stories with photographs of pretty girls go out over the country all the time is another factor to keep in mind when trying to estimate the future influence of this program.**

From Congressional Record, Jan. 4, 1929, p. 1166.

"When the command, 'Eyes right!' rang out on the old oval at Syracuse University, the optics of the student cadets of the R.O.T.C. snapped over with an audible click, for in the reviewing line were the newly installed and highly decorative co-ed sponsors." [14] By permission, *Syracuse N. Y. Journal*, 11/2/28.

POPULARIZER No. 3—PUBLIC DISPLAYS,
PARADES AND REVIEWS.

"The big parade for boy cadets where girl officers turn out to 'strut their stuff' is becoming a community event in many places and, of course, the Regular Army is glad to pull off these events, since it gives them opportunities to make speeches on the glories of preparedness and the general stupidity of our country in the past. You should see some of these gala parades and reviews held by our civilian training units—for the edification of those in the ranks and those in the grand stands . . . .

"These parades and reviews are made so thrilling and attractive by every means possible that the little tots of the community will look forward to the time when they get big enough to participate in yet bigger and showier parades."

Hon. Ross A. Collins, on floor of Congress,
1/3/29.

The headlines run:

"R. O. T. C. Units 'Strut Stuff' in Annual Review"

"They Did Themselves Proud Those Cadets".

"Boston Schoolboy Cadets, in Smart Parade Three Miles Long,

Thrill Many Thousands".

"15,000 at Gloucester H. S. Battalion's Field Day".

"Intermediate School Cadets Hold Their Competititve Drill".

"Reserve Officers Pass in Review Today Before Large,

Admiring Crowd".

"Pretty Sponsors Spur Boys in R.O.T.C. Annual Field Day."

"Major General Hinds Tells Denver High School Students

Another War is Certain".

"R.O.T.C. FLYING UNIT SOUGHT TO FIGHT PACIFISM

IN U.S. SCHOOLS."

"Efforts to establish flying units as part of the regular R.O.T.C. work at college, and to combat the efforts of pacifists who are seeking to undermine the national defense program of the U.S. are being made by Representative Melvin J. Maas of Minnesota, who is visiting San Diego on an aerial inspection trip over the country."

San Diego Union, 8/11/28.

PLAYING SOLDIER BECOMES A BIG SCHOOL AND COMMUNITY EVENT.

"Looking over Griffith Stadium as the Washington H. S. Cadet Corps waited at rest for the decision of the judges in the competitive drill."

Star Staff Photo.

By permission, *Washington* (D. C.) *Star,* 6/10/28.

"ELEMENTS OF MILITARY PSYCHOLOGY"
"By Commandant Taboreau

Extracts translated by
Major P. V. Kieffer, F. A., from Revue d'Infanterie."

* * * * * * "Our intellectual conditions, of themselves, do not urge us to action; **it is our state of sensibility, emotion, and sentiment** (affective conditions) **which are really the cause of our acts** . . . .

"**The sentiments are developed, like all human faculties, by use.** . . . **Sentiment is a chronic emotion.** Therefore, in order to cultivate a sentiment, the emotion which it expresses must be often experienced. This is why reading heroic stories, **applause of reviews,** discussing the greatness and the future of France develop the sentiment of patriotism.

"*****The use of ceremony is based on the law of psychology that our conscious conditions are intimately connected with our corporal attitudes; "**** Thus our gestures, our mimicry, our attitudes, even when mechanically assumed, are often able, to a certain degree, to incite in us the emotions to which they habitually correspond."

Coast Artillery Journal, Oct., 1928.

[16]

"PRETTY CO-EDS SHARE HONORS WITH R. O. T. C. UNIT AND BAND AT SEMI-ANNUAL REVIEW HELD IN STADIUM. Regiment and fair sponsors parade like veterans before Gen. R. H. Van Deman."

"The prettiest of San Diego high school's pretty girls had their place in the sun with the well-drilled R. O. T. C. Unit of the institution yesterday morning when the semi-annual review and presentation of sponsors was held in the stadium. Nino Marcelli, director of the famous high school orchestra and now director of the R. O. T. C. band, shared the honors of the day with the cadet corps and the girls, directing the band in the playing of his new march dedicated to Captain A. J. O'Keefe and the R. O. T. C. of San Diego.

"Distinction was given the occasion by the presence of Gen. Ralph Van Deman, commanding officer of the sixth infantry brigade with headquarters at Fort Rosecrans, who was present to review the regiment with the girls and then to review the girls as well as the regiment passed in review a second time with the pretty sponsors marching snappily beside the officers of the batallions and companies. . . . The regiment then passed in review before the Gen. Van Deman, the pretty line of sponsors, the regimental matrons, the principal, and vice-principal of the school and Marcelli. The regiment obviously took pride in its work and showed every evidence of careful and competent training.

"The batallion and company officers were ordered 'front and center', to be confronted by a line of girls equal in number to the officers. There was an instant of salute, and each officer claimed his sponsor and led her proudly to his unit where she took her position with as much mililtary precision as her escort. The companies and batallions greeted their sponsors with applause, and the band put down its instruments long enough to give a cheer for the pretty co-leaders. The crowd of high school students and towns-people who had turned out for the affair enjoyed the touch of self-consciousness shown by the young officers.

"The band marched and counter-marched, forming in front of the reviewing officer. Director Marcelli took the place of the student drum major and led the band in its new march. It was a stirring and tuneful composition which promises to be popular with the students when they have heard it a few more times and have become familiar with it.

"The band and Marcelli took the cheers and applause modestly and took position again, while the regiment passed in review once more, a middy girl marching snappily and striding along bravely with each cadet major and each cadet captain. Miss Henrietta Kishler, regimental sponsor stood in the reviewing line this time as did [list of ladies] the regimental matrons."

San Diego (Calif.) *Union,* 1/24/28.

[17]

"PICTURESQUE WAR"

" 'I suppose war is terrible, but isn't it picturesque?' " This is the remark made by a college student as she was watching the Armistice Day parade in her city. And one had to admit that the military spectacle was thrilling. Ex-soldiers in full regalia, camouflaged cannons, silk flags of special units and of the nation, military bands playing stirring airs—no one could watch the procession without being stirred. But stirred with a desire to reduce armaments? Stirred with a desire to sacrifice selfish nationalism on the altar of world peace? No, emphatically, no! Stirred rather with a sense of public pride in armaments, and a desire to exalt nationalism.

"The community celebration of the anniversary of peace served to make war attractive. The pageantry, the music, the spoils of victory, all tended to recall war and to surround it with glamor. The men who were parading knew that it was a false picture. They knew that modern war is not a gay affair of waving flags and beating drums and hearing the crowds shout 'hurrah!' They knew that modern war means anguish and torture of body, mind and spirit, beyond the reaches of the imagination of the cheering crowd. And yet, they were cooperating in an enterprise which made war 'picturesque.'

"College classes and public and private schools had been dismissed that morning to allow the young people and the children of the community to participate in a patriotic celebration. What did they learn from it? That patriotism is a matter largely of flag waving and shouting; that pride in America is bound up with military operations; that war is a thrilling romantic adventure. And the learning took place under such emotional conditions that months of patient teaching of the ideals of a Christian patriotism that strive for world peace cannot overcome its impressions.

"So long as our American communities continue to celebrate peace in such a way as to glorify war, sermons on world brotherhood, studies in international good-will, and compacts signed by great powers, will not be able to banish war from the earth.

"Youth loves adventure, loves thrills, and stirring experiences. Spectacular parades and oratorical speeches that recount the glories of war, are made the most important aspects of community holidays. The conclusion which youth draws is inevitable: War is a thrilling, romantic experience, an opportunity for high adventure.

"Cannot our communities teach patriotism of a truer type? Cannot respect and gratitude be shown to those who died in battle, without exalting war? Civilization moves forward. Mankind once knew no other way to settle difficulties than by combat. Individuals as well as nations fought to the death to avenge a wrong even though it was trivial. Individual disputes in stable communities have yielded to lawful settlement. Civilization is advancing from the period when gun powder and the sword afforded the only solution of a difficulty. Cannot our patriotic celebrations be prophetic? Can they not point forward to the day when patriotism and militarism will be completely dissociated, rather than point backward to the day when patriotism was interpreted almost exclusively in terms of fighting the enemies of one's country on the field of battle?

"Is your community, through its patriotic celebrations, teaching the children to love the habiliments of war? Then it is making remote the day when there will prevail peace on earth, good will among men.

Editorial, November, 1928. International Journal of Religious Education. Copyrighted, reprinted by permission.

POPULARIZER No. 4—SHAM BATTLES, WAR GAMES, FREE FIREWORKS.

"Thrilling Scene of Warfare Depicted by New York University Cadets in Review Before Army Chief."

R.O.T.C. Smoke Screen Hides Hall of Fame.

Wide World Photos.

While the children of the community enjoy the spectacle of higher learning and get the urge to be educated themselves.

[19]

POPULARIZER No. 5—PRIZES, HONORS AND AWARDS—

presented with proper display and publicity.

"With the civilized as with the primitive youth the 'game' is the medium of all successful training. 'Competition' is to youth what 'security' is to age."
Maj Gen. H. L. Scott, Chief of Staff U. S. Army, 1916.

"PRESENTING THE CUP"

"Miss Sarah Marshall handing the cup to Captain Frederick Mills for having the best all-round company in the Drexel R.O.T.C."—Acme Photo. *N. Y. Herald-Tribune, 6/12/27.*

"HONORED WITH SABRE. 'For service to his country'.. senior cadet officer ... is presented the Rotary Club sabre by ... president of the Rotarians, for outstanding work in the student army corps." *Syracuse Journal, 5/10/28.*

Military Contests and Prizes at University of Illinois.

The University Gold Medal.—The Trustees provide annually a gold medal awarded on Military Day to the best drilled second year basic course student, whose property the medal becomes . . . .

The Hazelton Prize Medal.— . . . a medal which is awarded to the best drilled freshman basic student . . . .

Cavalry Medal.— . . . a gold medal which is awarded, at a competitive drill . . . . to the best drilled cavalry student of the basic course . . . .

Infantry and Artillery Prize.—To the infantry company and artillery battery which win the competition . . . is awarded a silver cup.

Phalanx Award.—The outstanding freshman cadet in each Unit taking First Year Basic Course receives the Phalanx Award on Military Day.

Announcement in University of Illinois Catalogue, 1928, p. 75.

Thumb Nail Sketches*

"Girls Review Western High School Cadets."

"Company H, Fourth Regiment, Western High School Cadets (Washington, D. C.) drilling on Grounds at Friends School, are doing their best to impress Miss Edith Morris, Miss Jean Freling, and Miss Ann Shapiro."
Washington Herald, 5/11/28.

"Some rewards. R. O. T. C. Units of Boys' High, Tech. High, and Fulton High (Atlanta, Ga.) celebrated a **march in review with a bit of decorating** and accepted with becoming modesty the tributes of their fair admirers" (photo shows boy cadets lined up in row alternating with beautiful girls with bouquets.)
Atlanta Georgian, 5/3/28.

"Two Free Press Cups were among trophies awarded to winners of the ninth annual field day of the R.O.T.C. yesterday at Navin field. The four trimly dressed girls are sponsors of Central High School who were judged the best appearing."
Detroit Free Press, 5/30/28.

"Receiving the Captain Hathway Trophy from Mrs. Finley J. Shepard, after winning the individual competition in the manual of arms at the annual field day of N. Y. U. R. O. T. C."
New York Times, 5/27/28.

"Captain Macy of the High School R.O.T.C. receives $50 Prize and Sabre—to be awarded at the semi-annual drill and ball this evening."
New Bedford (Mass.) *Times,* 6/1/28.

---

*Clippings taken from beneath photos depicting the young heroes in their triumphs.

[21]

"OFFER 41 R.O.T.C. AWARDS."

"Eleven trophy cups and thirty medals to encourage proficiency in R.O.
T.C. work in Kansas City high schools were offered yesterday by the Heart
of America legion post.

"The cups will consist of one major trophy for general superiority in
unit records, and ten for special phases of unit performance. Three medals
—gold, silver and bronze—will be awarded the three best cadets in each
unit.

"Captain Harry E. Mitchell, instructor in charge of the R.O.T.C. and
Bernard Brannon, cadet colonel of the regiment, spoke before the post yesterday at its luncheon at the Hotel President....

"Captain Mitchell asserted R.O.T.C. activities were regarded at high
schools as a rival of athletics in interest."

Kansas City Star, 1/11/29.

"410 TEAMS WILL SHOOT FOR TROPHY"

"The number of entries in the 1929 National R.O.T.C. rifle match for
the William Randolph Hearst trophies has broken the records of all previous
years."

Washington (D. C.) Times, 1/17/29.

"CONGRATULATIONS flew thick and fast about the corridors of the
Calumet and Austin high schools today. 'The army', for the time being,
had attained the popularity it had enjoyed during 1917-1918, when to be a
soldier was to be 'sittin' on the world.

"For Austin high school's crack infantry platoon, commanded by Cadet
Major Frank Williams, had Saturday won for the school's trophy room The
Daily News shield for first place in close order drill. And at Calumet high
the student body flocked about Bertram Kent, 17, of 8506 South Peoria St.,
a member of the junior class and a color sergeant in the R.O.T.C. Kent
had been chosen not only as the best soldier in his school group, but the
best in the entire city as well.

"He will receive The Daily News medal as winner in this event, and
in addition will be given an autographed set of books by Maj.-General Paul
B. Malone, commanding officer of the 6th army corps area. In addition to
his army career, Gen. Malone has attained wide reputation as an author of
tales of army life."

The Chicago Daily News, 1/21/29.

"400 ATTEND 'U' MILITARY BALL AND DANCE. IN MARTIAL SETTING."

"ACCOUTREMENTS OF WAR BORROWED FROM SNELLING PROVIDE DECORATIONS FOR THIRTY-FIFTH ANNUAL AFFAIR; CRACK SQUAD DRILLS."

"IN A MILITARY SETTING, WITH SMALL CANNON, stacked rifles
and lighting effects simulating modern warfare, more than 200
couples, students of the University of Minnesota and their
guests, danced at the thirty-fifth annual ball, Friday night in
the ——. Army paraphernalia had been borrowed from Fort
Snelling for the ball. Outstanding in the evening's entertain-
ment was an exhibition by the crack drill squad of the University of Minnesota."

St. Paul Press, 12/8/28.

[22]

"THE INEXCUSABLE LIE"

"That was the morning I heard the Lie. **Of course I didn't know it was a lie.** How could I? My father told it to me, and I believed him. He believed it himself. He was quoting the words of his own father, his father's father. Fathers and mothers for centuries back had been repeating that Lie . . . . My father was talking. He told me so much—**marvelous stories. I thrilled again and again** . . . . The soft mold of my child mind took the impress deep, underlined, ineradicable. Gallant . . . glorious. Two words . . . wonderful! There was another word, soldier . . . and yet another word British . . . . prideful . . . .

"**Four words, and my childhood, youth, early manhood were colored, colored scarlet, to the martial echoing** . . . .

"My imagination came to life. **I wanted to be gallant and glorious too** . . . . My calculations did not get far beyond the picture I carried in my minds eye . . . . Logical. **First steps toward being glorious was to have the outward trappings of the position.** 'I want a uniform, Daddy'. . . . . I strutted about . . . . I would be a soldier, too . . . . I gasped out a demand for **tin soldiers** and **artillery** . . . . War, war, gallant, glorious! Pp. 39-43.

"My boyish mind could not read between the lines of romance the toll of mothers' broken hearts, fathers rent of ambition when sons are lost wives left to mourn, and children without food. P. 48.

"Generation to generation **we have carried war by tradition, by memory** . . . . **by inherited thought forces; war, a disease germ cultured in human mentality.** We have prepared the ground by vainglorious histories; propagated the deed by misleading bigotries, fertilized the virgin soil of youth's thoughts with the filth of national hatreds, saturated it with national contempts. We have stimulated the evil growth with scare headlines, a bought Press, hysterical outbursts of effervescent patriotism. **No wonder we have war,** the canker, the cancerous growth of a foul force. P. 36.

"**Is there not a mentality of war?** . . . I wonder, to have peace, will it not be necessary to teach the children Peace and not War? . . . "Why not tell, yes, you, **tell in one great word the truth of War,** the thoughts that follow and cry out—**cry out against all who teach the young to load and fire; to exalt the soldier and his trade;** to sing the glories of War; and **never a word of the bloody art of cutting throats.**" Pp. 13 and 10.

"The Inexcusable Lie," by Harold R. Peat.
Courtesy of Barse & Co.

"If instead of allowing their children to 'play soldiers', mothers and teachers would teach them St. Paul's saying, 'God made of one blood all nations', they would be helping the nations of the world to get together."
Lady Nancy Astor, reported in New York Telegram
1/17/29. Courtesy of the United Press.

POPULARIZER No. 6—HORSES—POLO.

"The young ladies are not the only agencies used in the Reserve Officers' Training Corps for the purpose of popularizing military training. Horses also play a large part. **There are certain schools that would probably not have a Reserve Officers' Training Corps were it not for the riding horses that are provided for the amusement of these young men.** Riding is becoming very popular socially, and most young men in schools like to ride, and **as long as they are able to ride a good horse, furnished, fed, and equipped in a fine splendid way by the United States Government, they join the Reserve Officers' Training Corps for the purpose of improving their horsemanship.** Nearly 2,000 horses are furnished now by the Government to various educational institutions, and additional ones were provided for in the 1929 bill and still more in this bill. The Government has 13 mules assigned to the Reserve Officers' Training Corps. I do not know whether there is any special significance in the number 13 or not, but I do know there is a dearth of mules. I presume that they are used for zoological purposes. . . .

"So you see we can now add to the saying 'Join the Army and become a man', 'Join the Reserve Officers' Training Corps and ride . . .' **The horse is kept in the Army because of its amusement and social value rather than its probable military usefulness."**

From debate in Congress on Army Appropriation Bill for 1930. Congressional Record, Vol. 70, No. 20, p. 1167.

AGAIN THE WAR DEPARTMENT DENIES RESPONSIBILITY FOR POPULARIZING.

Officers appearing before the Appropriations Committee of the House seem to give the impression the above is untrue. Note the testimony.

"**Mr. Barbour.** Right on that particular point, do they at some of the institutions use those horses to play polo?

Captain Watt. I could not answer that, Sir. They have to have polo ponies to play good polo. We do not provide polo ponies. They may exercise in that way by playing polo, and possibly use some of the mounts at the institution.

Mr. Taber. You have never heard of it?

Captain Watt. No, sir.

General Bridges. No, sir; because the horses furnished by the Government are not suitable for polo.

Mr. Taber. The Field Artillery horses are not suitable for polo?

General Bridges. No, sir.

Mr. Taber. How about the Cavalry?

Captain Watt. No, sir.

General Bridges. None of the horses we furnish to these institutions are suitable for polo, and therefore I would state almost positively that they do not use them for that purpose."

From Hearings before the Sub-Committee of House Committee on Appropriations, in charge of War Department Appropriation Bill for 1930, Part I. Page 885.

BUT LOOK AT THE REPORT ON NEXT PAGE.

"PRINCETON THE PIONEER IN COLLEGE POLO"

"Nassau's Four Horsemen of 1903 Constitute First Team in History. Establishment of R.O.T.C. Units Brings Post-War Renaissance to Game."

"In April, 1903, Princeton put the first college polo team into the field . . . . when the founders of the polo group left college, there was no one to carry the game along.

"Its present renaissance at Princeton and other colleges is due entirely to the establishment of the R.O.T.C. Courses, which make available for student use strings of government mounts, and the cooperation of the War Department in promoting the first of the intercollegiate polo tournaments.

"Major J. E. McMahon, U. S. Field Artillery, was the first commandant of the Princeton unit. In the late fall of 1920, although there were no facilities for polo, he managed to interest in the game a small group of students taking R.O.T.C. courses. At that time there were about eleven ponies among the artillery horses which were being used in the unit. These ponies had received no training for polo, but were of the polo type; and the men planned to start right away to train them as much as possible. Before the winter set in, they were able to do a little bit along this line, and then Major McMahon found an indoor ring at Trenton, eleven miles away . . .

"During the summer, a few more government ponies were obtained by trading in some artillery horses at the Fort Remount Depot . . .

"As our polo teams are practically under government auspices, the Athletic Association assumes no financial responsibility towards them, nor has any assistance ever been asked . . . . During the summer permission was granted by the Government for the shipment of twenty new ponies from the Remount Depot at Fort Reno, the Polo Association paying the freight. A group of officers spent the summer training these ponies so that they would be practically ready for fall practice . . .

"In 1925 and 1926 the University had erected a set of recitation buildings, stables, and gun sheds for the R.O.T.C. at a cost of $75,000. These were placed near the stadium and enclosed a space 300 feet long by 90 feet wide. Following the buildings' completion, private subscription afforded an additional $20,000, increased to $40,000 by the Trustees, for roofing the quadrangle and otherwise making a riding hall of it. The roof is of steel trusses, leaving the ring entirely free from upright supports, and there are two balconies capable of seating 500 spectators. Altogether, this indoor plant compares favorably with any in the country, and gives to riding and polo as an undergraduate exercise and sport all-year round appeal."

The Princeton Alumni Weekly, 1/25/29.

Does the War Department seriously believe that such expenditures of public funds add to our national security?

Will the next war be played on polo ponies or by skilled polo players?

Is this an honest effort at preparedness, or is it just making the military fraternity popular at Princeton and elsewhere?

What kind of citizenship and patriotism is this—getting or giving?

POPULARIZER No. 7—TONING DOWN THE TRAINING.

A PICTURE OF REAL MILITARY TRAINING

"It has already been said that the bayonet is one of the most important weapons of the infantry. *****

"The underlying idea of all infantry tactics is to close with the enemy as soon as possible and with all the units well in hand. ****

"**All the other details of an assault are to give the bayonet man an opportunity to close with the enemy** and the success of an attack depends upon, first, whether or not sufficient men can reach the enemy, and, second, having closed with him, **whether or not they are imbued with the spirit of the bayonet.**"

"Successful training implies that men will use on the battlefield what they have learned on the drill-ground. ****

"**The bayonet is the deciding factor in every assault** and the soldier must realize that its successful employment requires of him not only individual physical courage, but also perfect discipline and a thorough knowledge of teamwork. ****

"** The perfect confidence of the soldier in his weapon as required by his manual is the outcome only of long, continuous practice. To this end bayonet training will be kept up at all times except while actually in the trenches. ****

"**Do everything you can to encourage the men to practice with the bayonet,** training stick, etc., while off duty around barracks or camp, while at rest during other drills, etc. Utilize your own rest periods for short talks on the use and spirit of the bayonet. ****

"Bayonet fighting is possible only because red-blooded men naturally possess the fighting instinct. **This inherent desire to fight and kill must be carefully watched for and encouraged by the instructor.** It first appears in a recruit when he begins to handle his bayonet with facility, and increases as his confidence grows. With the mastering of his weapon there comes to him a sense of personal fighting superiority and a desire for physical conflict. He knows that he can fight and win. His practice becomes snappy and full of strength. He longs to test his ability against an enemy's body; to prove that his bayonet is irresistable. He pictures an enemy at every practice thrust and drives home his bayonet with stregnth, precision and satisfaction. Such a man will fight as he has trained—consistently, spiritedly and effectively. While waiting for the zero hour he will not fidget nervously. He will go over the top and win.

"*** an instructor's success will be measured by his ability to instill into his men the will and desire to use the bayonet. This spirit is infinitely more than the physical efforts displayed on our athletic fields; more than the enthusiasm of the prize ring; more, even, than the grim determination of the firing line—it is an intense eagerness to fight and kill hand to hand.***

"**In a bayonet assault all ranks go forward to kill or be killed, and only those who have developed skill and strength by constant training will be able to kill.** There is no sentiment about the use of the bayonet. It is a cold-blooded proposition. The bayonet fighter kills or is killed. Few bayonet wounds come to the attention of the surgeon."

Manual of Military Training by Moss and Lang, Vol. I, Ch. 29, prepared for and used in the R.O.T.C., but later supplanted.

IS THE R.O.T.C. MILITARY PREPAREDNESS OR MILITARY PROPAGANDA?

The layman can get some idea of what the War Department is aiming to do through the R.O.T.C., and of how far they are willing to go when he realizes that they prefer popularity to preparedness. This is shown better in their willingness to take the military value out of the R.O.T.C. work through toning it down and making it easy and pleasing than in anything else that has been done in this very extensive program of popularizing. One of the commonest arguments for military training is that it saves life in time or war. But how can this watered down training save life? The extracts from the R.O.T.C. manual quoted on the opposite page show an honest effort at picturing what is necessary for "success in battle." But when parents and citizens saw this realistic picture of preparedness they lost enthusiasm for military pursuits and began to talk about the necessity for removing such barbaric practices from modern life. Such realism in the training also exploded oft-repeated claims that military training is training in citizenship and character building. There was a wide protest against military training. Someone recalled the manuals in use, struck out the realism and, in January 1926, the War Department discontinued bayonet drill in the R.O.T.C.

Did the War Department remove bayonet drill from the R.O.T.C. because it wanted to save the lives of boys in the next war?

Is it possible that the whole war system might be repudiated by mankind if war and preparations for war were stripped of their glory and made to stand out in all their brutal realism?

PREPAREDNESS A LA R.O.T.C.

"**Mr. Collins.** Have you abolished bayonet drills at these universities and colleges?

Captain Watt. Yes, sir . . . .

Mr. Collins. Why did you abolish bayonet practice?

Captain Watt. I believe it was the general attitude toward that particular instruction.

Mr. Collins. It did not tend to popularize the work?

Captain Watt. No, sir."

Testimony before Sub-committee on Appropriations, of the House. dealing with the military appropriations bill for 1930. Page 920.

"The attack made upon the Organized Reserves and the C.M.T.C. by a contemporary service paper, which describes them as 'however remotely useful', is a direct criticism of the Regular Establishment, which is responsible for the civilian movement essential to our National Defense . . . . **the Army needs friends throughout the country, and those friends are found in the Reserve Officers and the boys who pass through the C.M.T. Camps. We are certain the pacifists obtain great comfort from the assaults our contemporary is making upon the R.O.T.C. and the C.M.T.C.**"

Army and Navy Journal, 2/16/29.

ADDITIONAL POPULARIZERS.

In a separate folder, "Brass Buttons in Education", we have shown how **the uniform, the arch beguiler of men and women down through the ages, is being used to popularize training in the colleges.** The War Department asked the last session of Congress for a thirty dollar uniform for the advanced course students in the colleges, to replace the four dollar and a quarter service uniform worn by the doughboys in France. They introduced testimony from college presidents to the effect that enrollments would be 40%-50% less in the elective, advanced course and opposition much greater where the training is compulsory if the boys were made to "serve" in the service uniforms of the doughboy. They were granted a $30 uniform for the advanced course. Then they came to the present short session of Congress (Jan. 1929) and asked for a $20 uniform for the basic students—and all the while men in the regular army, who will die first if there is another war, continue to serve in service uniforms.

Why is the War Department so anxious to please these boys who play at soldiering?

Another popularizer is **the common practice of presenting military training to parents and citizens as physical training, character building and training in citizenship.** One effect of this is to distract attention from the barbaric aspects and purpose of the training, while helping to keep alive our hero worship of the soldier as the highest type of leader, citizen and man.

Another very serious result is the tendency to substitute military work for physical education in our High Schools and Colleges. That means a distinct loss in manhood for peace or war. It is just one more way in which humankind is deceived by war and the trappings of war. Because the average parent does not know that military drill is not good physical training he is often led astray by this talk about "making men of the boys."

It is a sad day for democracy and international good-will when military men who have no particular training in pedagogy or in the subjects suggested are held up as master teachers of physical education, character building and the problems of citizenship,—just because they are military leaders. And yet this glorification of the army officer is going on all the time and military training is held up as a panacea solving all our educational problems—surpassing the combined powers of the home, the church, the school and other social agencies.*

The fact that **advanced course students are paid to take the course and are given a summer vacation in camp with pay, at federal expense** influences many poor college boys, who need the extra $100 per year, to elect military drill.

Often stress is laid on the point that free uniforms save clothes.

* For a complete discussion of the alleged educational benefits of military training see our pamphlet, "Militarizing Our Youth."

In many colleges, especially in some of the professional schools, the students are told that experience as cadet officers will be valuable training in managing (bossing?) workmen in industry and business.

Numbers of the colleges use their annual catalogs and announcements to draw rosy pictures of the advantages of the military work. (See our pamphlet, "The Camel and the Arab"). After hearing the statements made by some college authorities, on the sweeping results of the R.O.T.C., one almost wonders why they offer other courses—the military work gives such an all-round education.

Many colleges have local chapters of the honorary military fraternity, Scabbard and Blade. The members of this organization attain social distinction on the campus and often secure positions of prominence on public occasions which make membership a goal sought by many students who do not have favorable chances of "making" an athletic team or other "honors". Some college and high school administrations do what they can to make the cadet officers the "honor society" of the campus.

In at least three colleges the boys have had held up before them the patriotic (?) ideal of making the best of the next war, if there is to be one, by being officers rather than mere private soldiers.

Still other colleges have given the impression that military training is made mandatory by some authority outside the college and it is the student's patriotic duty to obey the law of the land.

Then there is the appeal to community or school pride and local patriotism. Students are asked to help put their school on the honor list or to help it secure distinguished rating. The War Department favors those schools and colleges where the administrations, the school paper and the student body "root for" the cadet corps.

And finally pressure is brought to bear upon those who do not join. Appeals are made to suppress criticism of the military idea on the ground that since the R.O.T.C. is a part of the college, criticism is "dividing the house against itself." This pressure upon students to join may take extreme forms. In the main corridor of Business High School in Washington, D. C., last autumn (1928) there was a large sign,

---

DON'T BE A SLACKER, BE A CADET.

"This nation's future, as far as war is concerned, will not be decided by the Department of State nor the government; it will be decided by the people. Today public opinion is ruling the nation."

Major Gen. Charles P. Summerall, reported in Bee News, Omaha, Neb., 11/27/28.

[29]

WHICH EDUCATION, THIS ——

"The University of Florida feels that in case war should come, it is preferable for its graduates to serve as officers rather than in the ranks."

Annual Catalog, 1927-28, p. 218.

"Let us not forget that the R. O. T. C. is to train our college men to be officers, not privates, in case of war. If some of the other states of the union plan things so that their college men will be privates, that is their apparent privilege." . . .

President W. W. Campbell, Univ. of California.
Address at the review of regiment, 12/7/25.

"Perhaps the greatest benefit of military training, however, is its training in the qualities of leadership. It is the only school subject that furnishes this practice. . . . It is also a selfish problem: In case of war, do you want to be a private or an officer?"

President Stratton D. Brooks, Univ. of Missouri. Address
to Univ. R.O.T.C., Columbia Missourian, 11/5/25.

"Our (military training) work stresses high standards in manhood and morality and I think this can be taught better in this work than in any other course of study. It stresses ability to think clearly, logically and analytically among the other essential qualities that are fundamental in the development of leadership."

President John Lee Coulter, North Dakota Agricultural College,
from a pamphlet issued by the American Legion, 1926.

"Armistice Day is Solemnly Observed in Calumet Monday . . . Early in the morning street flags waved from their positions along the streets calling attention to the spirit of patriotism which imbued those who laid down their lives in France ten years ago to make this day a reality and an anniversary of the triumph of righteousness . . . Colonel W. P. Moffett commander of the Calumet high school R. O. T. C. gave a brief but interesting talk on national defense, pointing out the necessity of preparedness to insure continued prosperity . . . 'Preparation for war is the best means of preventing war'."

Morning Gazette, Calumet, Michigan, 11/13/28.

"Our great country was conceived in war, nurtured in war, and preserved by war."

Major General Charles P. Summerall, in address
at East Providence, R. I., 7/30/27.

"Kaiser Still Clings to Ideal of Force . . ." . . . diplomacy only is effective when there is a unified will backed by force . . . Whoever wants to dictate to the world with the pen alone will not do it unless supported by the keen edge of the sword."

Review of "My Ancestors" in N. Y. Times, 1/21/29.

—— OR THIS ?

"What, then, is the place of military education or military training of American youth? We should like to say that there is no place in this age of advanced education, which recognizes the supremacy of humanitarian ideals, which recognizes the mutual dependence of the nations of the earth and their peoples upon each other, which recognizes the brotherhood of all races and creeds, that enlightened nations can acknowledge as such" . . .

"The ideals of the kind of obedience and of general conduct aimed at by military exercises are best represented by the word 'martinet', which these exercises long ago contributed to our educational vocabulary—ideals which every teacher who aims at real character-development, seeks to avoid.

"Those who favor military drill maintain that it is the most effective means of developing patriotic feeling. . . . But if we look beneath the surface, we find that military patriotism may be no deeper and no more lasting than military obedience."

Report of the Committee on Military Training of the Department of Superintendence of the National Education Association, School and Society, 3/31/17.

"We need have no war unless we wish to. It depends entirely upon our free will . . . . The disarmament of the war forces of armies and navies is very important, and we must do what we can to further it. But if we would work really efficiently for peace among the nations of the earth we must begin from within . . . it is the disarmament of the human mind, of the soul of peoples."

Dr. Fridtjof Nansen, reported in New York Times, 2/19/29.

"Military training is primarily a device for making boys into soldiers. It cannot and does not make good any other of the educational claims made for it. It should be judged solely for what it is, a training school for the prosecution of war, and hence for the continuation of national distrust and hatred. And as such, it can have no place in an educational system designed to achieve world-citizenship."

William G. Carr, "Education for World Citizenship." P. 131.

"War between two great civilized nations does not break out suddenly. It is the result of a state of nervous tension, irritation, and fear in the minds of the inhabitants of the potential enemy nations. First there is a growing accumulation of fear and resentment, the atmosphere becomes explosive and a tiny spark explodes it. . . . And behind the creation of this international feeling leading to the outbreak of war lies ever one emotion—fear. Fear of what? Fear of war. . . . In the Middle West suspicion of England can still be made an election issue. . . . Students of international affairs should take note of the ease with which a modern democracy can be stampeded into the state of mind that sets it shouting for war.

Lt. Commander J. M. Kenworthy in "Peace or War", p. 108.

"When the Pennsylvania State Art Commission went on record as refusing to approve the use of cannon in the future as war memorials, another shot was fired at the goal of world peace!"

Christian Science Monitor, 11/23/28.

[31]

"THE PSYCHOLOGIST LOOKS AT THE ARMY"
A Presentation of the Practical Relationship Between Psychology and the Profession of Arms.
by Captain John H. Burns, Infantry."

" 'Civilization has harnessed to the use of war the primitive forces which are as old as man; rhythm, vanity, herd instinct and rallying instinct. Their symbols are the fife and drum, the uniform, the regiment, and the flag. Against these the peace mongers storm in vain, for they are deep in human nature and can never be eliminated.'—Carter: Man is War.

"Members of the human family massed in crowds display characteristics quite different from those they display as individuals **** He (man) is more sensitive to the voice of the herd than to any other influence. **** It is the source of his many codes, including the military code ***.

"**The military problem, psychologically speaking, resolves itself into taking every advantage of the herd instinct to integrate the mass ****. This military processing of civilians is a purely empirical thing, but it is an eminently sound one. It has been handed down from past armies. ****

"It is useless to try and convince men of the value of military standards by reasoning with them, for reasoning, no matter how brilliant or conclusive, always leaves a suspicion of doubt and uncertainty in the mind of the average man. It is necessary that he be firmly convinced, and the best way of doing this, in fact the only way, is to indoctrinate him. **Constant repetition of the item to be inculcated, unsupported by any reasons, will have an immense effect on the suggestible, herd-minded human.** An opinion, an idea, or a code acquired in this manner can become so firmly fixed that one who questions its essential rightness will be regarded as foolish, wicked, or insane. Suggestion, then, is the key to inculcating discipline, esprit, and morale. This may throw some light on why such qualities can not be formally taught, but seem rather to be by-products of military experience and formal instruction.

"***** anything that makes a man conscious of his membership in a herd, and at the same time proud of the herd, is an important integrating factor. Many of the distinctive features of military life owe their existence to the fact that they are such factors.

"***** Parades and reviews are great factors in securing unity. **For with pomp and glitter the great unit is massed, and to the sound of rhythmic music with flags flying and cadenced step the sub-units pass and render homage to their commander.** For the soldier not to be conscious and proud of his identity with his herd is, under these circumstances, almost impossible. Finally, to express its unity the herd is given a symbol—the colors.

"But probably the greatest tool in the hands of the officer for bringing home to the members of the group their basic unity is close order drill.**** **Three things, then, are fostered by close order drill; one, the growth of herd consciousness; two, the development of the habit of automatic obedience; and three, the recognition and acceptance of leaders, and the belief that these leaders have herd approval behind their actions.** ******

"No process of military training, however, can succeed completely unless the material turned over to the military has been indoctrinated with certain ideals of duty, patriotism and citizenship. **Men who have absorbed in childhood the belief that war is the greatest disaster, that nothing justifies it, and that it can always be avoided;** men who believe that military leaders are rather to be pitied than praised, *** such men are not good soldier material. **They will never make an army.** ******

"**The national army's training begins in the nation's schools. It is** spiritual in character."

By permission, *The Infantry Journal*, Dec., 1928.

[32]

"MEN MUST DISARM MINDS"

"That Is Real Way to Peace, Explorer Declares at Meeting or Economic Club."

"Lauding the Kellogg Treaty as a 'step in the right direction', Dr. Fridtjof Nansen, explorer, issued a plea last night at a dinner of the Economic Club of New York, at the Hotel Astor for 'disarmament of mind' as the real way to world peace . . . .

"Dr. Nansen described his experiences as High Commissioner of the League of Nations in charge of repatriation of prisoners of war to illustrate the horrors of such tremendous conflicts. 'That is what war really means,' he said, 'but people seem to forget easily and now you hear some of them talking in a light hearted way about the next war . . . .'

" 'It is not so much physical disarmament as disarmament of mind that is needed. We must educate young people to understand how to work for humanitarian ends and not to work for war'."

New York Times, 1/30/29.

"I look upon the Hon. Mr. Kellog's pact to outlaw war not only as a legal convention binding the various peoples, but as an advance in civilization that will, as I trust with confidence, save mankind from future wars. This pact points the way which civilization is bound to take, if advance and not collapse is to be the final goal—the way of peace and harmonious co-opeation of the nations. The German people are eager and willing to proceed in this direction."

Dr. Gustav Stresemann, Foreign Minister of Germany,
St. Louis Post-Dispatch, 9/19/28.

"In every country today there is much direct schooling of the public mind into acceptance of war as a legal and, in certain circumstances, desirable thing, by the naval and military chiefs. When Lindbergh, the heroic air-mail Atlantic flyer, returned to the United States, great efforts were made to exploit him as an advertisement for American naval and military flying . . . . I have referred to the popularity of military parades and displays. Since the war this method of glorifying militarism and representing only the pride, pomp and circumstance of war has been reduced to a fine art . . . . These parades of troops are spectacular and magnificent, but they are not War. But the simple-minded people are apt to think that they are War . . . . The parade ground movements provide a spectacle for the people but they are utterly unlike anything that would be attempted on the field of battle. It would be more honest if the troops marched in battle kit, their faces hidden in the hideous modern gas masks. But this might bring home the reality of war. It is only its romantic side that is presented . . . . If this is not glorification of war generally and the preparation of the public mind for the next war, there is no meaning in the words of the English language."

Lt. Commander J. M. Kenworthy in "Peace or War," p, 182.

"So it is high time that the spiritual forces of humanity united in a determined opposition to the warlike spirit which finds expression in the council of the greatest democracy of the modern world. We used to think that war was the sport of kings. It is in great danger of becoming the toy of democracies. There is as much danger in the jingo spirit, the demagoguery and the loose talk of delegates in the congresses and parliaments as there used to be in the rattling of sabres by monarchs."

Hon. George W. Wickersham, reported in N. Y. Times, 2/19/29.

[33]

"Fair Sponsors of the Hill R.O.T.C. ... Officers of the Syracuse University R.O.T.C. with women student sponsors of the unit."

By permission, *Syracuse Herald*, 11/1/28, Photo by Arthur Cornelius, Herald Staff.

RECRUITS FOR WHAT? ——

"One hundred and fifteen students have enrolled in the R.O.T.C. this semester at Polytechnic high school as a result of a very efficient publicity campaign, conducted by a number of the Poly officers.

"While this number falls far short of the goal set by the recruiting officers, it is a considerable increase over last term's enrollment. The campaign was conducted in an effort to secure 200 cadets, which would have made Poly eligible to compete for the title of 'honor school.'

"This rating is awarded annually, following the federal inspection by the Ninth corps area inspector. Those schools having 200 or more cadets present the day of the inspection who have the loyal support of the student body and who have a well trained unit are awarded the title.

"Many activities have been indulged in by the cadets, and more are in prospect. Last Thursday evening was R.O.T.C. night at a downtown showhouse. More than 600 cadets from the schools of the city were the guests of the management of the theatre, Eddie Peabody, who is an honorary member of unit, and the Poly battallion . . .

"The cadet corps has always been one of the most important of Poly's organizations."

Los Angeles Herald, 2/18/28.

FOR THIS? ——

"A warlike spirit, which alone can create and civilize a state, is absolutely essential to national defense and to national perpetuity . . . . the more warlike the spirit of the people, the less need for a large standing army, as in such a community every able bodied man should be willing to fight on all occasions whenever the nation demands his services in the field.

"In a free country like our own where everything depends upon the individual action of the citizen, every male brought into existence should be taught from infancy that the military service of the Republic carries with it honor and distinction, and his very life should be permeated with the ideal that even death itself may become a boon when a man dies that a nation may live and fulfill its destiny."

Maj. Gen. Douglas McArthur in Infantry Journal, March, 1927.

—— OR THIS ?

"The world has never advanced, commercially, intellectually, socially, morally, or spiritually by conflict between nations. Decisions that are arrived at by the sheer power of physical force, have no rational basis, nor have they ever been acceptable to the best thought of the world. They have merely aroused the instinct of brute passion, hatred, jealousy and revenge. Therefore, we charge ourselves with the determination to labor energetically against all efforts to perpetuate war-like ideas. Especially do we condemn the institution known as the Junior R.O.T.C. in the high schools, and the compulsory phase of military training in the colleges and universities of our land."

From report of the first merged conference of Illinois Churches, giving the Methodists' stand, Peoria Journal, Sept. 18, 1928.

WHAT ATTITUDES ARE WE POPULARIZING—
THESE ? ——

"When the people of one country, through the education of its youth, come to understand the ideals, aspirations and the hopes of other countries, then they no longer will submit to war, any more than a civilized community now will tolerate a street brawl."

Dr. Uel W. Lamkin, Pres. Natl. Education Assn., speaking to State Convention of Mo. Teachers. Kansas City Star, 11/15/28.

"It is better a hundred thousand times to be beaten over an arbitration case than to be victorious in a modern war. That is the lesson we have to learn and to teach . . . . . let us highly resolve never by one jot or tittle to promote the cause of wars, or to make men believe in the necessity of the ordeal by battle. If we can but cultivate the Will to Peace at home and abroad the great fight for peace will be won . . . . I am confident that the will to peace is growing and that the common sense of the peoples will make it finally victorious over all obstacles."

Sir Esme Howard, British Ambassador to America, speaking to 106th Infantry Regiment in Brooklyn, 11/13/28.

"If the people are minded that there shall be no war, there will be not be. Arbitration is the machinery by which peace can be maintained. It cannot function effectively unless there is back of it a popular will for peace . . . . There is one other means that can be taken by governmental authorities and by private organizations like yours throughout the world, that is to inculcate into the minds of the people a peaceful attitude, teaching them that war is not only a barbarous means of settling disputes, but one which has brought upon the world the greatest affliction, suffering and disaster."

Secretary of State, Frank B. Kellog, speaking on Armistice Day, 1928.

"We are all determined that the curse of war shall not again devastate nations. The most certain insurance against this is the training of the thoughts of men in the ways of peace."

Secretary of State Kellog, in letter to General Convention of Episcopal Church, 10/21/28.

" . . . . a new force . . . is rising in all its grandeur for the outlawing of war . . . . —the irresistible expression of the well considered opinion of the world to cease armament for defense of its treaties . . . . 'Have we not now advanced to the point where national wars can be banished from the earth by the power of public opinion? . . . The war showed us that in future wars there can be no victors and vanquished—there can only be the vanquished, all involved in that stupendous ruin' . . .

"The only way mankind can escape that prospect is through the swelling force of public opinion that in years past has ended feudalism, 'trial by battle' and duelling."

Myron T. Herrick, American Ambassador to France, speaking to World War Veterans in Cleveland, Armistice Day, 1928, reported in Cleveland Press, 11/12/28.

"Once the nations have repudiated the baneful and immoral right of war against one another—as they have done—it is hopelessly illogical to go on preparing for war."

Viscount Cecil, former British Minister, in special statement to New York World, 2/4/29.

—— OR THESE ?

"GEN. ELY SAYS WAR CANNOT BE BANNED. Peace treaties and the League of Nations may delay but will not abolish war, in the opinion of Major General Hanson E. Ely, Commander of the Second Army Corps Area . . . . at the weekly meeting of the New York Rotary Club. . . . 'That they (the peace covenants) will cause war to cease is beyond the brain power of human beings . . . . We don't prepare for war, but against it. As long as we have reasonable national defense, an adequate army, a good navy and a sufficient air force, so long will we be able to prevent war, and no longer. . . . If we had now or could get together . . . . more tanks, airplanes and munitions than any other country, and faster than any other country, we could lay our cards on the table and say, 'There is our hand, can you beat it?' And there would be no war'."

Reported in N. Y. Times, 9/21/28.

"We all know there will be a next war, despite talk of peace pacts . . . There is no necessity for this country to be unprepared for the next war. . . We can get around these disarmament pacts and be prepared for the next war only if we adopt some sort of program to maintain industrial prepared-ness."

Gen. Hanson E. Ely, at Exchange Club of New York City, reported in N. Y. Times, 10/12/28.

"GEN. ELY ATTACKS PEACE ADVOCATES. 'Half-baked students in our colleges, led by half-baked presidents' were the objects of a slashing attack by Major General Hanson E. Ely . . . at the Central Y.M.C.A., Brooklyn."

Brooklyn Daily Eagle, 3/9/28.

"SEES AMERICA FIGHTING WORLD. James F. Archibald, famous war cor-respondent and adventurer, in addressing an assembly of R.O.T.C. cadets at the University of California at Los Angeles predicted that the next war will bring the United States against the world."

Madera (Calif.) Tribune, 12/27/28.

"MCNUTT SAYS GUNS SURPASS GOOD-WILL TRIP. South American coun-tries 'can hear the sound of a gun farther than anything else'. Paul V. Mc-Nutt, national commander of the American Legion, said last night in a ref-erence to President-elect Hoovers' good-will trip . . . Mr. McNutt's sentiments had been seconded before he made them by Mrs. Boyce Ficklen, Jr., national President of the Legion Women's Auxiliary, when she said her organization had no patience with those who clamored for 'friendships, not battleships'. 'Battleships make friendships sure', she said. To this Mr. McNutt nodded in assent."

Baltimore Sun, 1/11/29.

"Diplomacy is only effective if there is a nation in arms behind it ready to enforce its will . . . . Notwithstanding good diplomacy, only might creates respect for the interests of one nation by other nations."

The Ex-Kaiser in "My Ancestors," reviewed in N. Y. Telegram, 1/21/29.

[37]

"SHE COMMANDS THREE HUNDRED MEN"

"Meet Colonel Dorothy G. Stone, Commanding Officer of the University of Kansas Reserve Officers' Training Corps Unit. Colonel Stone is the ranking officer of the corps at parades, reviews, drills, formations and ceremonies. She is also charged with looking after the social affairs of the military battalion."—P. & A. Photo. *Detroit Free Press*, 1/20/29.

SOME QUESTIONS FOR PARENTS AND CITIZENS:

Is it safe to associate the greatest thrills of youth with the military machine and with those who are by duty bound to preach the military philosophy of life?

Is it wise to use such sales methods in securing recruits for patriotic service on the field of battle?

Do we want such military shows, especially in the High Schools, to become the big event of the year in our American communities?

Will a genuine opposition to war and the trappings of war be built upon such a pleasing preparation for war?

Is this training in patriotism and citizenship? Do such sales methods make for an accurate evaluation of the real merits and objectives of the R.O.T.C.?

If this is not enthroning the military "game" and the military caste in the minds and hearts of our youth, what would?

Is such playing at war a frank attempt at military preparedness or is it just keeping the war "game" alive and attractive?

STUDENTS !

Shall we allow the army to sell us military preparedness and their brand of political philosophy as we are sold tooth-paste, cigarettes, or movie thrillers?

Are our High School and College youth willing to be the actors in a show that will take the sting out of thoughts of war and make younger boys and girls look forward anxiously to the time when they can be a part of this play-at-war-machine?

Does such playing at war make for an educational approach to the war-peace problem?

If we sell ourselves to the war machine for a little fun and a few dances are we free to decide the real issues of peace and war on a factual basis?

Are these Girl Colonels the kernel of the argument for snappy uniforms for the advanced course? (See our pamphlet, Brass Buttons and Education, where we quote Major General Charles P. Summerall as saying to the Military Appropriations Committee, "The principal concern during the past year has been in connection with the uniform," with regard to the R. O. T. C.)

Are our pretty girls willing to be used as billboards for the military machine and the military philosophy?

Is it fair to young men to drag them into the clutches of Mars with girls as bait?

IS THIS WAR ?

"LITTLE CO-ED COLONEL"

"Miss Leslie Walters was selected out of fifty pretty candidates at South Dakota State College to be honorary cadet colonel of the R.O.T.C., and lead the grand march at the annual military ball. Eight other college girls composed her staff." P. & A. Photo.

Atlanta (Ga.) *Journal,* 12/23/28, etc

WE BELIEVE:

1. These methods of popularizing the military show the determination of the military-minded to keep their method alive.

2. Calling military training under such circumstances and incentives "patriotic service" is mixing motives—if not perverting patriotism.

3. Enlisting interest in military preparedness and attracting recruits for training by such methods obscure the purpose of the training and conceal the stark realism of war—weakening both preparation for war and opposition to war.

4. Making membership in the military establishment so appealing to personal motives will lead to a growing membership in and increasing support for such—without regard to the social and political needs for or results of the military.

People do what they like to do—and find the reasons later. When it is such fun to be in the R.O.T.C., boys and girls can find plenty of good "reasons" to support their presence there—and these will be "high-sounding" reasons.

5. This is really enthroning the war method and the war machine in the lives of our people. When boys and girls enjoy such thrills and build such strong personal associations around the military establishment and military officers they cannot do their part in uprooting the old mental habits and prejudices which keep war alive.

Preparation for war is made thrilling—the whole experience of the trainee builds an emotional halo around his association with military life.

6. Most people support the groups in which they find themselves and the attitudes expressed by the group without any critical examination of those attitudes. If our "gang" thinks it is so, it is so. Enrolling our boys and girls in the military fraternity, makes them unconscious supporters of that viewpoint.

7. Introducing such glorified playing at soldiering into our High Schools is particularly bad. These young people are even more subject to such appeals than adults and become easy victims of war psychology. Being too young for serious military work, they are simply turned into boosters for the National Defense Act and the military machine.

8. The time has come when parents and citizens must stop this linking of the program of the military-minded to the personal ambitions and sentiments of our youth. Humanity has reached the point where we can and must kill the "inexcusable lie" that war is glorious and inevitable.

"Trained youth cannot take the place of trained manhood. **Youths make imitation, but not real soldiers.**"

Major General L. H. Scott, Report of Chief of Staff U.S.A. 1916

LADIES, HAVE WE COME TO THIS?

"Woman Militia in Every State Planned by Sex. Legislation to Create Feminine Auxiliary of National Guard to be Asked Soon"

"Mrs. C. Fuller Winters, president of the American Federation of Industrial Women, says the woman's guard bill will be introduced soon . . .

" 'Women will be eager to enlist in the woman's guard for reasons both of health and patriotism. There will be regiments in every State, proportioned to balance with the regular National Guard.'

"Mrs. Winters said the bill would put the guardswomen under the War Department. Officers of the regular army or National Guard would be detailed to train the guardswomen until they could select their own leaders.   ......

" 'The training at first would necessarily have to be moderate, but later women could be trained into work of the cavalry, infantry, artillery, air corps and other branches of the military service,' she said.

. . . ." 'already thousands in business life and society have indorsed the movement' . . . . .

"Mrs. Winters said a tentative uniform for the Woman's Guard has been designed. It includes riding breeches covered by a split skirt, puttees, O D. skirts and a specially designed close-fitting turban hat.

" 'The Woman's Guard, in addition to military training, would provide physical training that every woman in America needs. It would also offer discipline' she said.

" 'Women for years have been pampered by men; the men don't realize it, and neither do many women. This causes many failures in life, both in the business world and socially. Military discipline would greatly correct this evil.' "

New York Telegram, 12/1/28.

"POLO AT COLLEGES FOUND TO BE CHEAP"

"Corvallis, Ore., Feb. 26, (A.P.)

"Polo, called the most expensive American sport and calculated to cost $10,000 for each individual per season, in reality is inexpensive as a college sport.

"Figures compiled at the Oregon State College disclose that the total outlay for a team at those schools where the Government maintains cavalry R.O.T.C. need not average more than $150 per season. It makes polo decidedly less costly than the run of minor sports at a college.

"At Oregon State the only expense is for transportation and that is paid from receipts earned at the games. There is no expense for a coach as the army furnishes a man who has regular duties in the R.O.T.C. in addition to the coaching.

"The Oregon State mallet swingers are allotted two ponies, Regular Army horses, which are used in riding classes. Their original cost would not average $166. They are cared for by enlisted soldiers so there is no additional expense for grooming. The saddles and harness are Regular Army issue. To the polo club mallets are about the only expense.

" . . . Using these army horses, Oregon State last year was able to tie Stanford for Pacific Coast honors."

New York Evening World, 2/25/29.

[42]

THIS PREVENTS PROGRESS TOWARD PEACE.

If another great war comes, it will be in spite of the economic interests and general welfare of the mass of mankind; and because of their sentimental attachment to certain methods of feeling and action. The man on the street who is swayed against his own welfare to rush blindly into his own destruction is one of the danger spots of the world. Mental disarmament is necessary.

Many assume that military training is harmless if it does not make people want war, or make them like war. No considerable number of people anywhere in modern times have "wanted war." Wars do not come because the mass of men "seek them," but because the mass of men do not definitely dispense with them in favor of other means. The mass is still led to believe that war is inevitable and that preparedness is the only way to peace. This belief is bolstered up by powerful emotions which blind men to all logic and fact. Men's feelings are at least as important as their beliefs, in causing war.

This watered down and popularized military training may or may not prepare boys to defend their country in war, but it certainly does keep alive these old emotions. And keeping alive these old emotions guarantees that war itself shall be kept alive.

Mental disarmament is impossible while "playing at soldiering" is such fun.

The effect upon the life of a community of having such displays of the military within its borders is well brought out in *A Study of International Attitudes of High School Students*, by Dr. George Bradford Neumann, published by Teacher's College, Columbia University, as one of its contributions to education. Please remember that the situation described in the following quotation shows the effect upon students who merely lived in the same community with a military academy, but were not enrolled in that academy.

"Possibly the most interesting of all those mentioned is the last one given, the two schools being Staunton and Charlottesville. Both are in Virginia and comparatively close to each other, but their environment has certain suggestive differences. It will be noted that on many items they agree in tendencies where such tendencies are different from those expressed in northern schools, but in this particular instance they have a significant difference between themselves. Possibly the character of the content of the item affords the clue, for it is to the effect that **the highest type of patriotism makes us willing to fight for our country, whether it is in the right or in the wrong. On this Staunton emphatically expresses its approval, while Charlottesville is as emphatic in opposition.** The same direction of tendencies is seen in the responses to the last item of the indicator (D45) to the effect that it is unwise and unnecessary for us to spend hundreds of millions of dollars each year for military preparedness. To this Charlottesville responds with a mean of 3.90, very close to the point of indecision, while Staunton's **mean response is 3.20, which places it in the area of strong negative attitudes.** Apparently there are some strong influences which **make Staunton more militaristic than its neighbor, and the presence of a famous and popular military academy at Staunton is a reasonable hypothetical explanation.**"

IS THIS INNOCENT CHILD'S PLAY?

Some may ask, "After all is this not just the innocent play of children—the natural thing to expect from growing boys and girls?" It is innocent so far as the intentions of the young people are concerned, and for that matter the purposes of most of the adults connected with military training are quite innocent.

The young people are very innocent of any desire to cause a war, or to see a war. It seems quite logical from the incentives offered to attract these recruits that they are even innocent of any strong desire to prepare for war. Their experience in the cadet corps leaves them pretty "innocent" of the real nature of war and of serious preparation for war. The philosophy and military history given in the courses, by direct teaching and by suggestion, leave these boys and girls still "innocent" and ignorant of the causes of modern wars.

The parents also are quite innocent in their aims. Every mother wants her boy and girl to be at the head of the parade of life. She and they will grasp at every opportunity to attain the coveted positions, prizes, distinctions, and attainments of their community. The presence in the community of a military unit offering all the advantages claimed for such, and illustrated in this pamphlet, presents to the ambitious parent and child, to the average person, a very fruitful field for endeavor—a very playground of attractive spoils. We should not be surprised if most young people and their parents enthusiastically accept "the game of soldiering" and try to excel in it. They are innocent—guileless.

Because many military men and many of the advocates of the training are just as thoroughly unaware of the part psychological forces—deliberate and unconscious, beliefs and feeling—play in bringing about wars, they too are innocent in urging this innocent "playing at soldiering" upon our youth.

Innocent? Probably,—but for that reason, all the more harmful. Just because it seems to be "such a natural thing to do," "such a fine chance for a boy," this "playing at preparedness" is much more dangerous than a frank, cold-blooded attempt to teach people to seek war and to enjoy it. Such a program would be quickly recognized for its true nature and crushed, because men do not seek or enjoy the realities of war. (Witness the protests and subsequent dropping of bayonet drill.)

The fallacy lies in thinking that any body of men do "want war" or "like war", and that wars arise for that reason. Wars come out of stored-up, hidden beliefs and sentiments,—emotions and attitudes people are unaware of, or they would uproot them and denounce them. The emotional results of keeping alive these hidden forces are the real dangers. That they are unforseen and non-deliberate makes them even worse. To make the immediate aspects of preparedness so pleasing as to blind men totally to the ultimate realities and results of the system of accepting war as forever inevitable is suicidal. **Sugar coating this social fatalism which accepts war as inevitable with appeals to personal ambition will retard just that much the growth of new attitudes, and a new adjustment to the world as it really is.** The war system, now long past its practical usefulness, can survive only when bolstered up by such sentimental crutches. This innocent play with such explosive material as our human emotions may be guileless and innocent but it is tragically out of date.

WHO IS RESPONSIBLE?

In attempting to fix responsibility for international ill will and conflict **we cannot excuse those who bolster up these old habits, innocent though they may be of any deliberate, purposive attempts to do wrong.** Passing all responsibility for international strife onto the shoulders of other nations is sheer folly. We must look within our own group for those attitudes and practices which make our nation one of the two parties necessary for a quarrel.

For this reason **we must very definitely fix responsibility for this program of popularizing the military idea, the military man, and the military establishment**—and for the fatal results which must surely follow if we keep up this practice—**upon those who advocate popularized training.** Agents of the War Department, Reserve Officers, and civilian groups that foster this "playing at soldiering" will be just as truly responsible for the gradual militarizing of our youth, which must inevitably follow this practice, as if they were "bloodthirsty" or did "want war". **The deadliness of the poison being poured into the life of our people is lessened none by the fact that it is not labelled "poison".** The party of intoxicated youths who go for a mad, joy ride in a fast machine, and subsequently destroy themselves are just as dead as if they had deliberately set out to commit suicide. Giving our youth this fatal old toy, military glory, to play with will accomplish the same results for our civilization.

POPULARIZING IS INCREASING

Some have expressed the hope that the practices we have been describing would defeat their own ends—because they are so ridiculous. Unfortunately a study of the field shows that they are not only on the increase, but "popularizing" is becoming more popular. Colleges and High Schools that started out three or four years ago with one or two girl officers have eight to twelve now. In the beginning some schools merely had these girl officers appear at the annual military ball; now they appear also at reviews and inspections. The number of High Schools and Colleges using girl officers grows steadily. The number of stories and pictures appearing in the press increases each year. The absurdity of the practices and the more absurd press stories that go out do not prevent new recruits from seeking the publicity to be had.

The story on page four of the "hard boiled little Colonel" illustrates the powerful pull of these positions even when the publicity secured does present the girl officer in a ridiculous manner. The girl officer described has vigorously denied the interview carried in this story, and protested to us that it was a ridiculous caricature. However this lampooning of her did not prevent the R.O.T.C. at that institution from appointing another girl Colonel this year; nor did it prevent that Colonel from posing for a large photographic syndicate which has circulated her photo more widely than that of her predecessor. Along with it has gone a story of the work of the girl officer which is even more laughable than the one we print. It credits her, for example, with "looking after the morals of the cadets". So long as we offer such attractive plums to boys and girls, if only they will advertise the military, we shall find the system growing.

DECEPTIVE PREPAREDNESS

The practice is all the more indefensible because of the fact that "popularized" training and "camouflaged soldiering" possess so little value as real military preparedness. One can have great respect for the honestly held viewpoint that great military preparedness is the only sensible course for mankind; but one must ask serious questions about the attitude that converts this earnest business into a game. One may disagree with the view that big preparedness saves life, but one must respect the party who earnestly and sacrificially works for that goal. **But is this a frank, honest and sacrificial preparation for service?** In an editorial discussing the various measures before Congress when our present National Defense Act was finally adopted, the Army and Navy Journal (issue of 4/24/20) has this to say:

"Another question, and even more important than that of the cost . . . is the length of time in training that should be required . . . .

"One of the commonest and weakest arguments advanced in the universal training cause is that 'preparedness' saves the lives of men. That statement is true only to a very limited extent. The men of the German army at the outbreak of the war were prepared for warfare, and yet they were killed in appalling numbers. The original British expeditionary force was unquestionably better prepared than any army that left England to engage in war. Von Tirpitz said of the enlisted personnel of that force that they were all sergeants', by which he meant that they were the finest and most experienced type of soldier. Yet they too were killed to an extent that shocked the allied world. If military training is to save the lives of men, no such results can hope to be achieved by the short terms of training proposed in the (pending bills which provide for 3 or 4 months of training) . . . ."

Real military preparedness is a serious business and should be presented as such, if we are to follow the policy. **This playing around with High School boys and girls is not preparing men to act as defenders of the nation. So far as it has any results it is largely preparing them to think like soldiers.**

"Back of every effort to train and discipline an army properly is preparation for battle. . . . It is the properly organized, trained and disciplined army that fights like a fiend and brings home victory."

Chaplain Milton O. Beebe, Coast Art. Journal, May, 1927.

THE WAR DEPARTMENT HOLDS ANOTHER CONFERENCE TO "PROMOTE NATIONAL DEFENSE"

We opened this pamphlet with a brief description of the conference held at the call of the Secretary of War in 1922. As we go to press we receive the story of a new attempt to enroll popular support. This time it is a conference of ladies.

"WOMEN GIVEN PART IN NATIONAL DEFENSE"

"War Department Approves Plan To Name Contact Officer"

"A system of coordination between various women's organizations and the Department of War in order to promote national defense, was announced by the Secretary of War, Dwight F. Davis, February 25.

"The announcement followed a meeting on February 25 of representatives of various women's organizations with Secretary Davis. The meeting was held, Secretary Davis explained, as the result of continued demands on the part of women to have some part in the civilian work of national defense. They believed, Secretary Davis, said, that they have as much right to participate in these activities as the men.

"Accordingly it has been arranged, Secretary Davis stated, for the appointment of a woman as chief contact officer between the Secretary of War and the women of the country. She will be aided by representatives in the nine corps areas of the United States and in the Philippines, Hawaii, Porto Rico and the Panama Canal Zone.

"These women, Secretary Davis said, will act personally and not for their organizations, although it will be their duty to secure the cooperation of all women's organizations.

"Secretary Davis said that some of the women had brought up the need of combating pacifist propaganda of other women's organizations. He denied, however, that this was the purpose of the organization and maintained that all that was necessary was education in order to combat pacifist propaganda.

"When asked whether the new women's representatives will have officers in the Department of War, Secretary Davis said that they would cooperate through Miss Anita Phipps, Director of Women's Relations, Department of War. They will probably have the right to use stationery and will receive a certificate signed by the Secretary of War, he stated.

"The women are now considering the appointment of their chief and of their corps representatives, Secretary Davis stated."

United States Daily, 2/26/29.

"All history shows that armaments do not prevent wars. Allied to the peace-by-terror party are those who think that if only a nation is armed to the teeth she will be able to escape war. The most heavily armed nations in Europe were those involved in the last war. This school of thought is addicted to the quotation of Scripture. They are fond of citing the 21st verse of the 11th chapter of the Gospel according to St. Luke, which reads as follows: 'When a strong man armed keepeth his palace, his goods are in peace.' But they omit the next verse, which reads as follows: 'But when a stronger than he shall come upon him and overcome him, he taketh from him all his armour wherein he trusted, and divideth his spoils'."

Lt. Commander J. M. Kenworthy in "Peace or War," p. 291.

RE STUDY THESE CONTRASTS AND CONTRADICTIONS:

This pamphlet has been prepared to help church groups, women's clubs, teachers, students, parents and other citizens interested in building the habits of peace, in their effort to estimate the probable results of military training.

The Committee on Militarism in Education, of which Dr. George A. Coe is the Chairman, is concerned with the problem of breaking those habits of thought and feeling which make war possible. Speakers, further literature on the subject, suggestions for opposing militarism in education are supplied on request. Your support is needed.

Copies of this pamphlet will be furnished at cost: 1 copy, 15c; 12 copies, $1.25; 50 copies, $4.; 100 copies, $7.; 1,000 copies, $50.

Published by

COMMITTEE ON MILITARISM IN EDUCATION

387 BIBLE HOUSE, ASTOR PLACE

New York City